ADMIT ONE

McGraw-Hill Reading

Wonders

McGraw-Hill Reading Wonders

McGraw Hill Education

Bothell, WA • Chicago, IL • Columbus, OH • New York, NY

Cover and Title Pages: Nathan Love

www.mheonline.com/readingwonders

The McGraw-Hill Companies

 Education

Copyright © 2014 The McGraw-Hill Companies, Inc.

All rights reserved. No part of this publication may be
reproduced or distributed in any form or by any means, or
stored in a database or retrieval system, without the prior
written consent of The McGraw-Hill Companies, Inc.,
including, but not limited to, network storage or
transmission, or broadcast for distance learning.

Send all inquiries to:
McGraw-Hill Education
Two Penn Plaza
New York, New York 10121

ISBN: 978-0-02-119511-4
MHID: 0-02-119511-0

Printed in the United States of America.

7 8 9 10 QVS 17 16 15 14

C

McGraw-Hill Reading Wonders

CCSS Reading/Language Arts Program

Program Authors

Diane August	Jan Hasbrouck
Donald R. Bear	Margaret Kilgo
Janice A. Dole	Jay McTighe
Jana Echevarria	Scott G. Paris
Douglas Fisher	Timothy Shanahan
David Francis	Josefina V. Tinajero
Vicki Gibson	

McGraw Hill Education

Bothell, WA • Chicago, IL • Columbus, OH • New York, NY

Animals Everywhere

(b) Dana Hursey/Masterfile

THE BIG CONCEPT

Figure It Out

Go Digital! http://connected.mcgraw-hill.com/

Together We Can!

Go Digital! http://connected.mcgraw-hill.com/

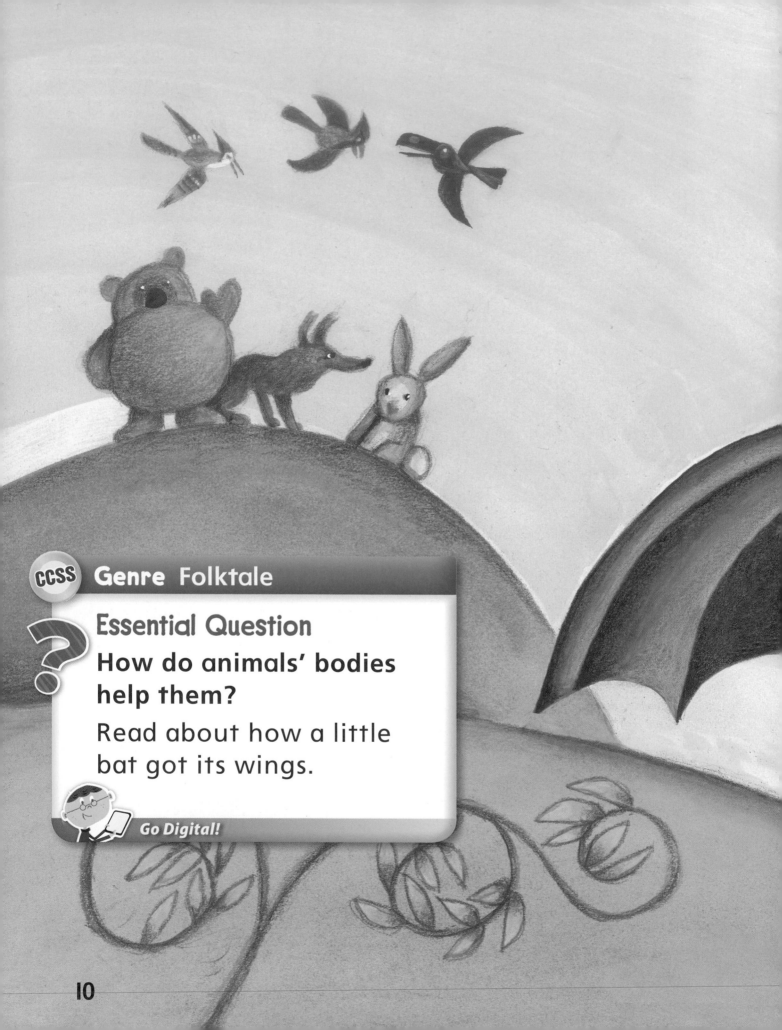

Essential Question

How do animals' bodies help them?

Read about how a little bat got its wings.

Go Digital!

How Bat Got Its Wings

retold and illustrated by
Gerald McDermott

A long time ago, the **animals** had a big game of ball.

They broke up into teams. One side had birds, or animals with wings. The other side had animals with legs. But they did not have wings.

The animals who did not have wings were big and fast. They could toss a ball a long way and run like the wind.

The birds were fast but not as big. Yet with their wings, they could **carry** a ball way up in the air. The animals with legs could not jump up and grab it.

At last, game day came. The animals
and birds met on the playing field.
Both teams felt very excited.

"We will win!" came the calls.

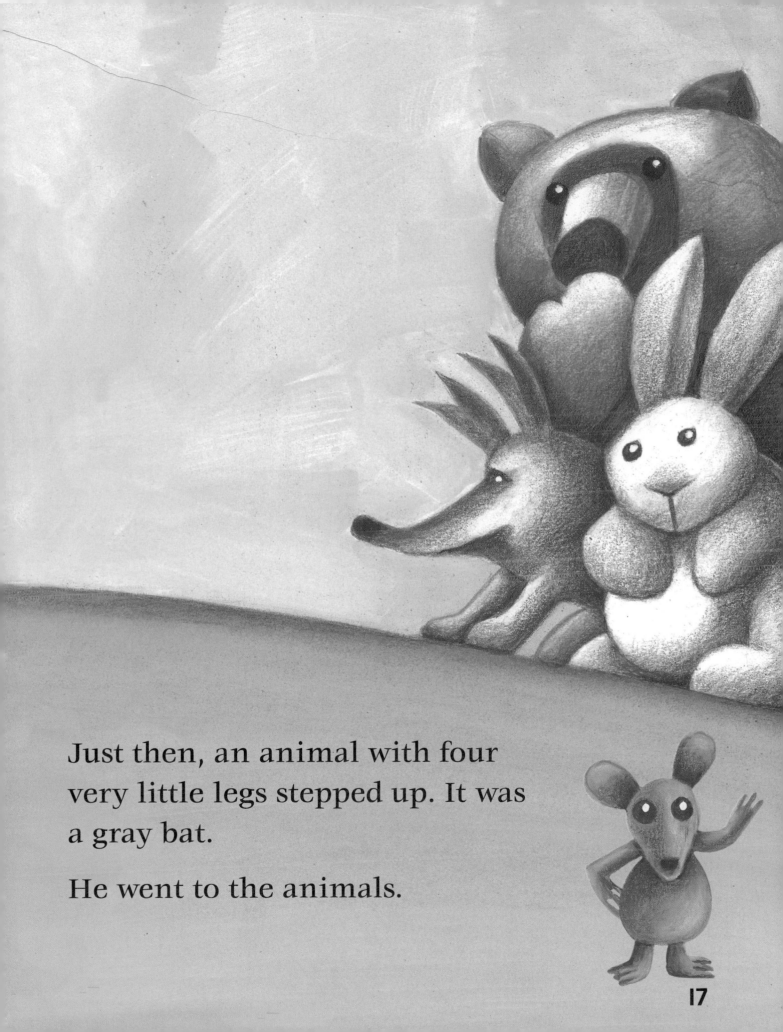

Just then, an animal with four very little legs stepped up. It was a gray bat.

He went to the animals.

17

"Can I play on this team?" he asked.

"You are much too small to play," laughed the animals. "And look at those little legs. We can't win with you!"

"I may be little," said Gray Bat. "But I can do lots of things."

Next, Gray Bat went to the birds.

"Can I play on this team?" he asked.

The birds shook their heads. "**Our** team has wings," they explained.

"But the animals say I am not big and can't play with them," said Gray Bat.

Then Blue Jay spoke up. "Maybe there is a way for Gray Bat to play with us."

"Tell us **about** it," said Raven.

"We can **give** him wings!" said Blue Jay.

"That is **splendid**!" Cardinal exclaimed.

So the birds took the skin off the top of a big drum. Then they took sticks and made **special** wings for Gray Bat.

"Let's see if he can fly," said Blue Jay.

Gray Bat flapped his wings.

He went zig and zag. He could not go in a line like a real bird.

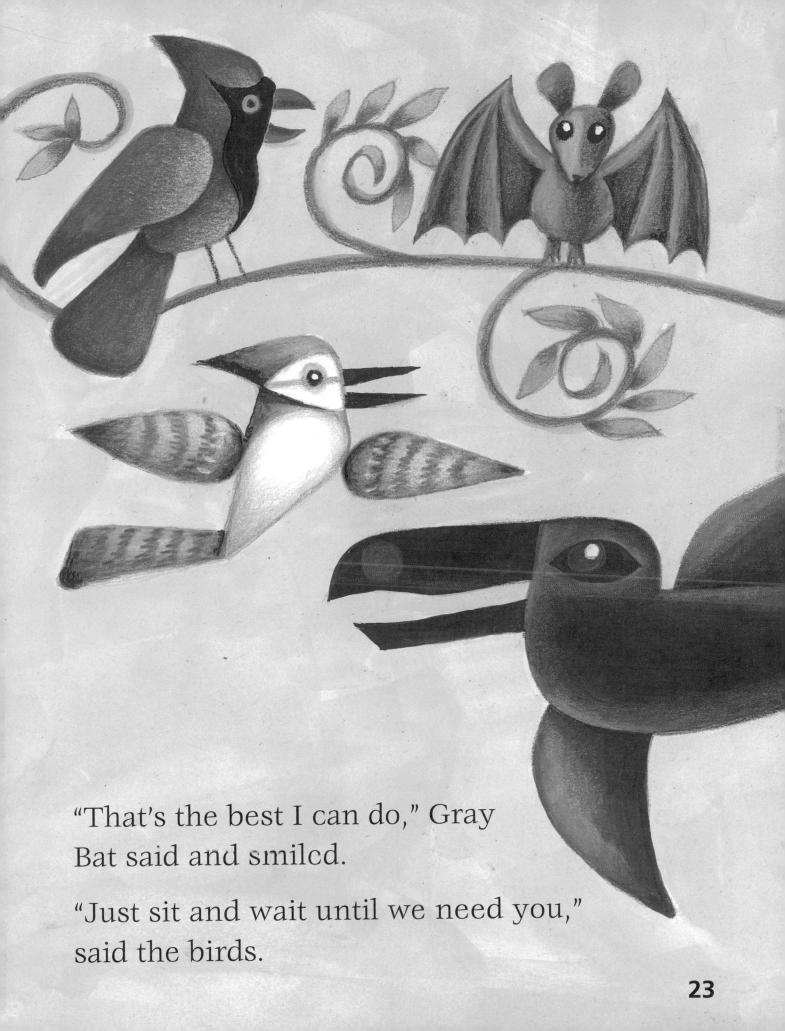

"That's the best I can do," Gray
Bat said and smilcd.

"Just sit and wait until we need you,"
said the birds.

At last, the game began.

The animals and birds played their best to win. The ball zipped up and down.

Gray Bat just sat and waited.

When the end of the game was close, each team had **eight** points. Gray Bat still had not played.

With a little time left, the animals took the ball and ran with it.

Just then, Gray Bat stood up.

"Let me help," he said.

He flew up, up, up with his
special wings. He grabbed
the ball and carried it in his
zig-zag way. The animals
could not catch him.

"We win!" yelled the birds. "Gray Bat did it!"

To this day, Gray Bat plays on the bird team. He flies in his own way.

And that is how the bat got wings.

About the Author

Gerald McDermott says, "Animals, animals, animals! I love to draw them jumping and hopping and flying across the pages of my books. You can draw animals, too!" Gerald McDermott has illustrated folktales starring interesting animals from all over the world.

Author's Purpose

Gerald McDermott wanted to retell an old folktale. Think of a story about an animal. Draw the animal in your story. Write about it.

Gerald McDermott

Respond to Reading

Retell

Use your own words to retell *How Bat Got Its Wings* in order.

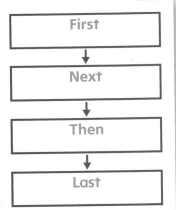

First
Next
Then
Last

Text Evidence

1. What happens when Gray Bat asks to play with the birds? **Sequence**

2. What is the last thing that happens in the story? **Plot**

3. How can you tell that *How Bat Got Its Wings* is a folktale? **Genre**

Make Connections

Think of an animal you know. How could it use its body to help win a game? **Essential Question**

Bats! Bats! Bats!

A bat is a special animal. There are more than 1,200 kinds of bats. A bat can be black. It can be white. It can be gray. It can have spots. The biggest bat has a wing span of 6 feet!

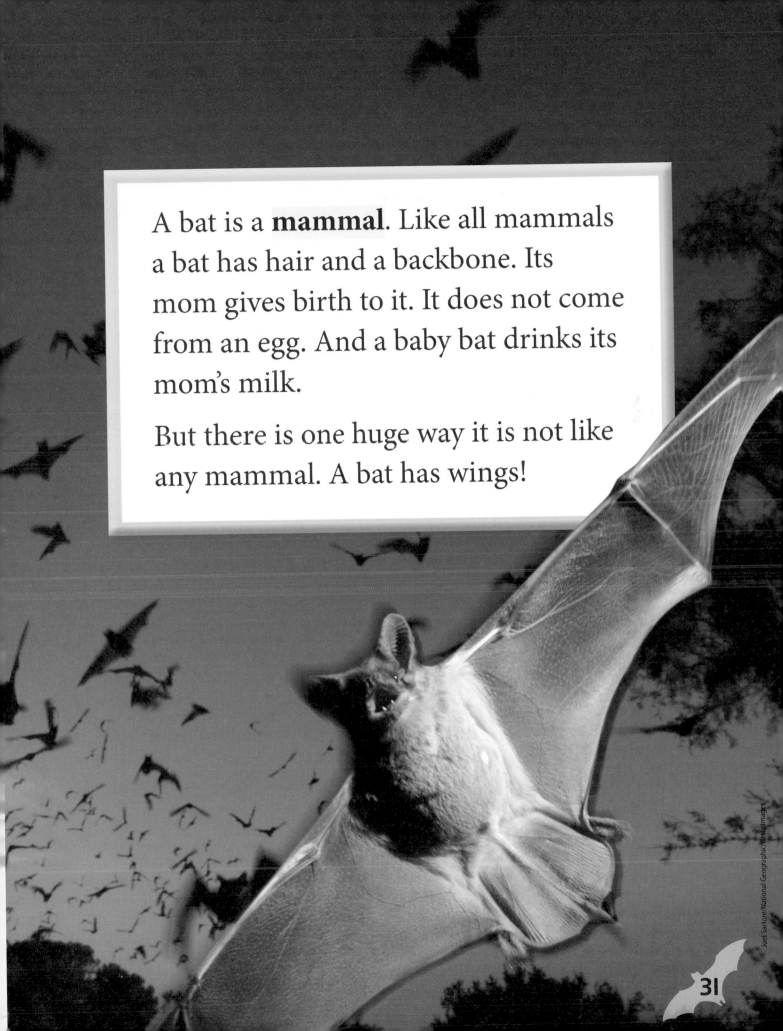

A bat is a **mammal**. Like all mammals a bat has hair and a backbone. Its mom gives birth to it. It does not come from an egg. And a baby bat drinks its mom's milk.

But there is one huge way it is not like any mammal. A bat has wings!

Bat or Bird?

Body Part	Bat	Bird
Ears	Big ears to hear at night	No big ears, but has small holes on side of head
Covering	Fur (hair)	Feathers
Wings	Two wings made of thin skin and hair; four fingers and a thumb on each wing	Two wings with feathers
Legs	Two short legs with claws	Two long legs with claws
Nose	Big nose that comes in many shapes and sizes	No nose, but has a bill, or beak

A bat is the only mammal that can fly. But it is not a **bird**.

Look at the chart. It tells the ways a bat and a bird are the same and different.

Bats like to make homes in caves and trees. These homes are called roosts. Lots of bats live together in a roost.

It is daytime. But the bats stay at home to sleep. They like to hang upside down.

At night, the bat wakes up and **hunts**. How does a bat get food when it can't see? A bat makes a sound. When the sound wave hits something, an echo bounces back. The echo tells the bat if something to eat is close.

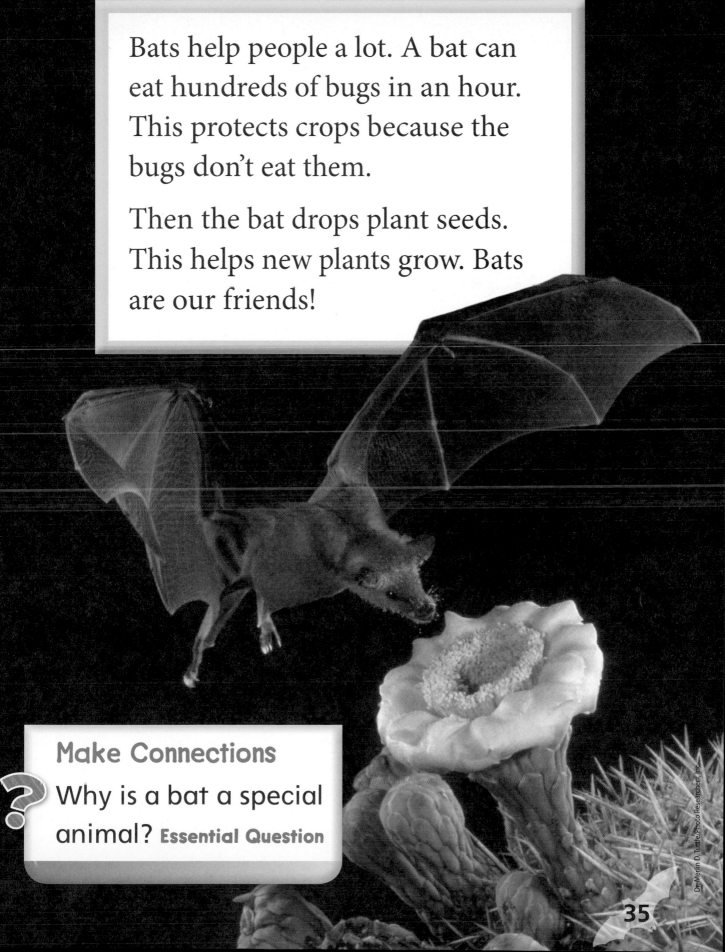

Bats help people a lot. A bat can eat hundreds of bugs in an hour. This protects crops because the bugs don't eat them.

Then the bat drops plant seeds. This helps new plants grow. Bats are our friends!

Make Connections

? Why is a bat a special animal? **Essential Question**

Dr. Merlin D. Tuttle/Photo Researchers, Inc.

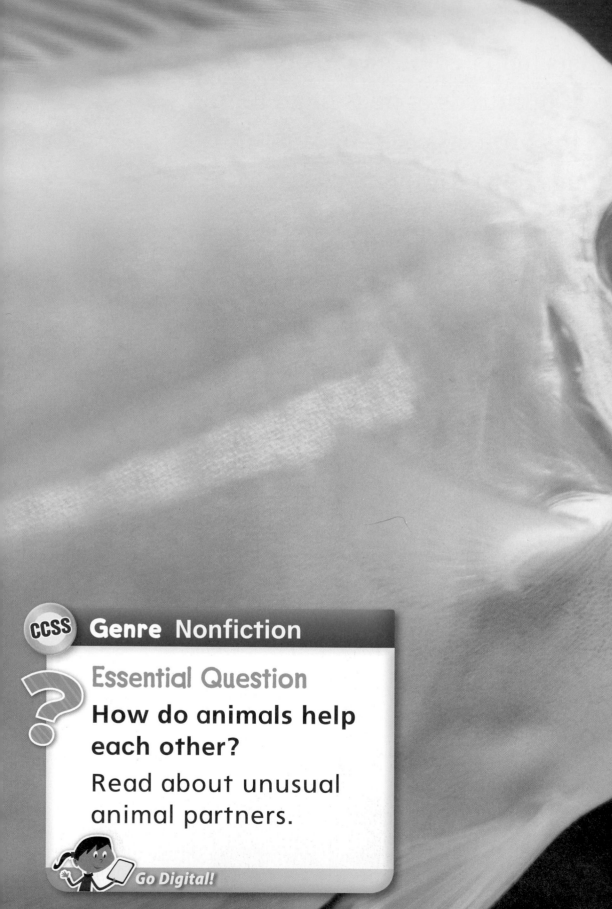

CCSS **Genre** Nonfiction

Essential Question

How do animals help each other?

Read about unusual animal partners.

Go Digital!

Animal Teams

by Rachel Mann

Can a **small** bird help a big giraffe?
Can a shrimp help a fish?

Yes, they can!

These may seem like odd friends. But many animals work together in teams. These animals help each **other** in lots of ways. Let's find out how.

Some birds live
off the backs of
big animals. Why
do the animals
let the birds stay?
The birds help.
They eat bugs off
the animals' skin.

The big animals help the birds, too. They keep the birds safe. And it is a good deal for them **because** they have lots of sweet bugs to eat!

The goby fish and the blind shrimp make a good team.

The shrimp can't see, so the goby helps. The goby looks out for **danger**, and the shrimp stays close. When the goby flicks its tail, it means that it is time to hide.

The shrimp helps the goby, too. It will go **into** a hole to hide. It lets the goby hide here, too. The shrimp and the goby hide until it is safe to go out.

(br) Oceanwidelmages.com

43

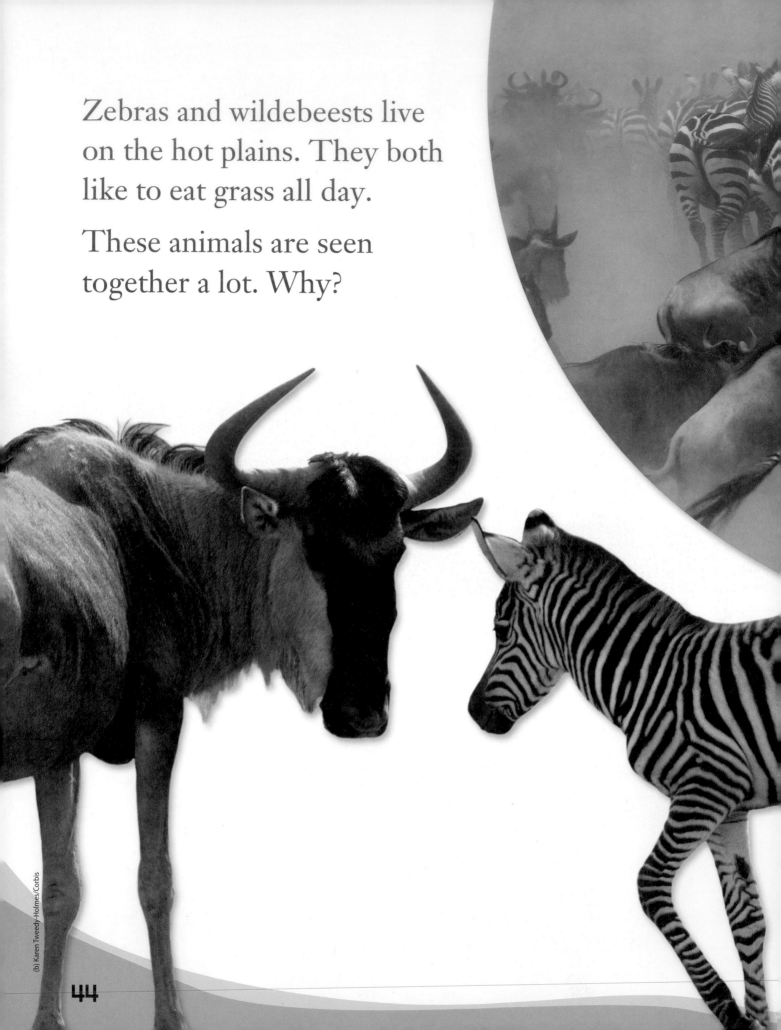

Zebras and wildebeests live on the hot plains. They both like to eat grass all day.

These animals are seen together a lot. Why?

They stay together because they can help each other find fresh grass to eat.

They also help each other keep safe. If a zebra **or** a wildebeest spots danger, it runs. This tells the rest to run, too.

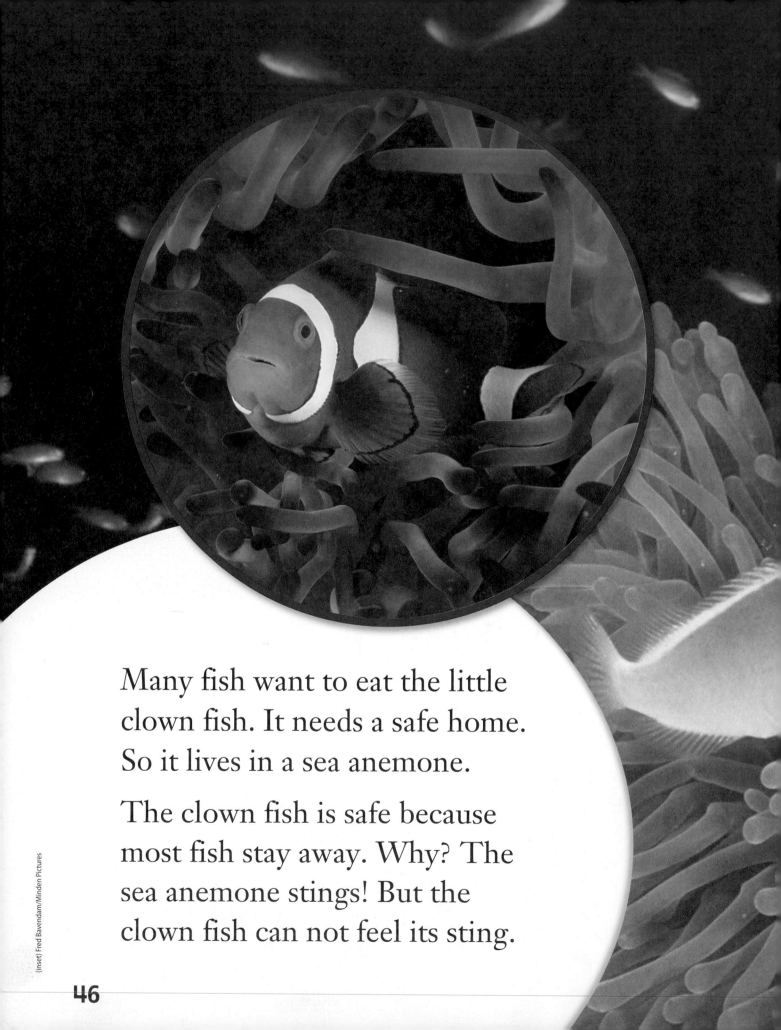

Many fish want to eat the little clown fish. It needs a safe home. So it lives in a sea anemone.

The clown fish is safe because most fish stay away. Why? The sea anemone stings! But the clown fish can not feel its sting.

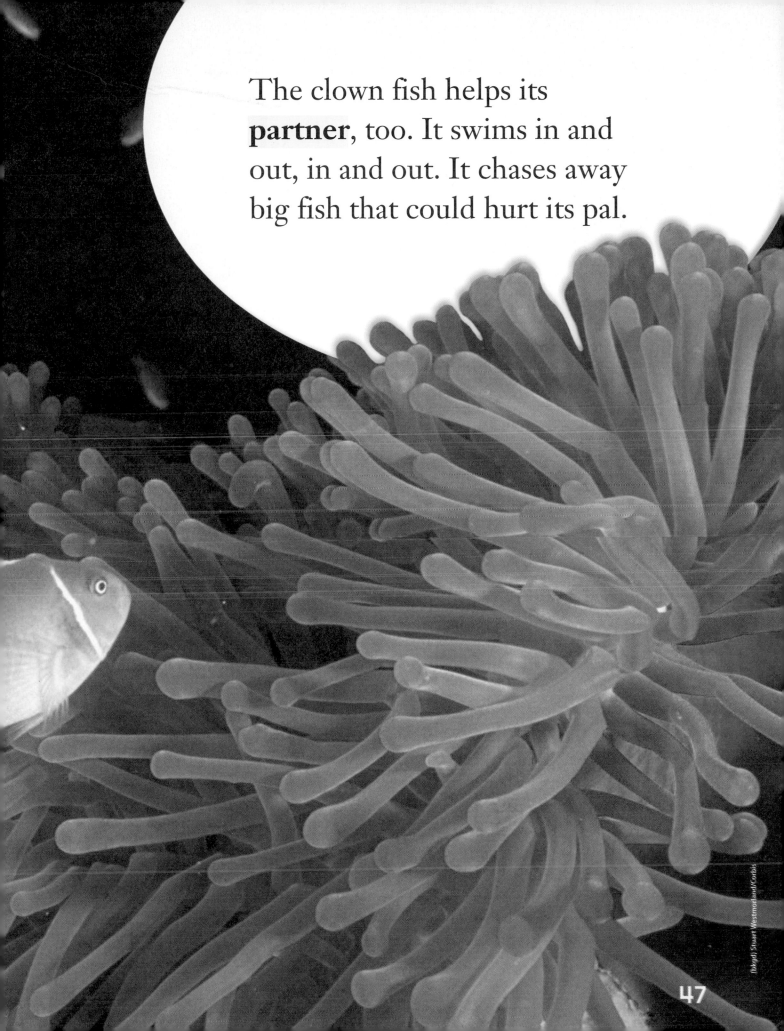

The clown fish helps its **partner**, too. It swims in and out, in and out. It chases away big fish that could hurt its pal.

A caterpillar needs to be safe so that it can grow.

Who will help? Ants will! Ants see the caterpillar and take it to a safe place.

Why do ants do this?

(b) Arco Image GmbH/Alamy

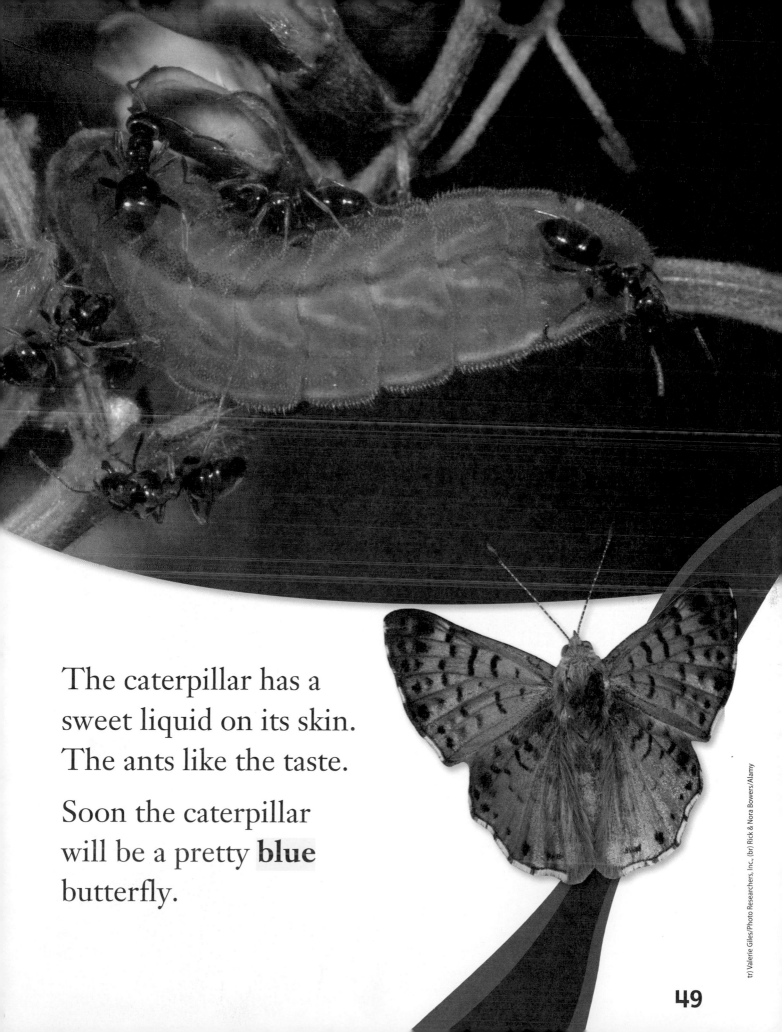

The caterpillar has a sweet liquid on its skin. The ants like the taste.

Soon the caterpillar will be a pretty **blue** butterfly.

When a little cleaner fish wants to eat, it looks for bigger fish to clean. Why? It gets a free meal when it cleans.

A cleaner fish eats the pests off of other fish.

The big fish want to be cleaned! They line up and wait for the cleaner fish to get to them.

One is big, and one is small.
But the two are a team.

When animals team up, they do what
is best for both of them.

Meet the Author

Rachel Mann loves learning about animals, especially animals who act in unexpected ways. She really enjoyed researching and writing *Animal Teams*, because she learned that animals help and need each other just as people do.

Author's Purpose

Rachel Mann wanted to write about animals who do interesting things. Write about an animal that does something you find interesting.

Respond to Reading

Retell

Use your own words to retell the important details in *Animal Teams*.

Text Evidence

1. What is the main idea of *Animal Teams*? **Main Idea**

2. Why do some birds sit on the backs of big animals? **Details**

3. How can you tell that *Animal Teams* is nonfiction? **Genre**

Make Connections

What animals have you seen together? How did they help each other? **Essential Question**

Compare Texts

Read about how bees work as a team.

Busy As a Bee

Bees can make a hive in a tree.

Bees are at home in a hive. All of them have jobs that help the hive.

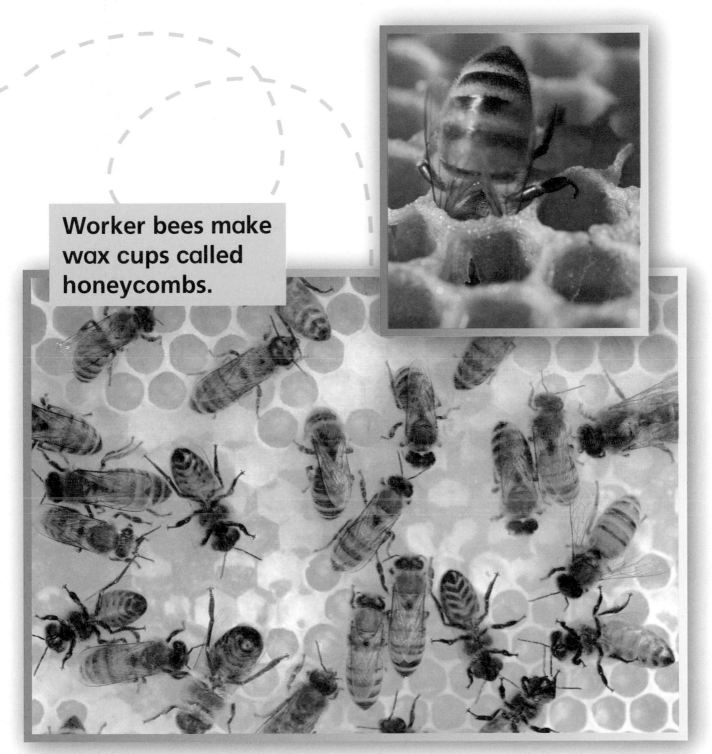

Worker bees make wax cups called honeycombs.

Lots of **worker** bees help make **honey**.
They help keep the hive clean, too.

Every hive has a **queen** bee. She lays all the eggs.

A hive has drone bees, too. A drone's job is to help the queen make eggs.

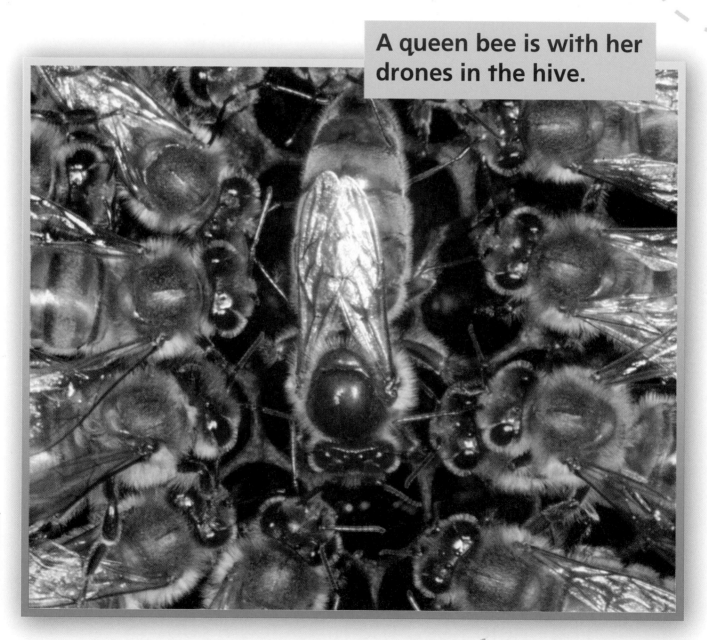

A queen bee is with her drones in the hive.

The queen lays eggs inside wax cups.

New bees hatch from these eggs.
Worker bees feed them.

A big hive is a busy place!

Make Connections

How are the bees like the animals in *Animal Teams*? **Essential Question**

CCSS **Genre** Nonfiction

Essential Question

How do animals survive in nature?

Read about how a very unusual animal gets its food.

Go Digital!

Vulture
View

by April Pulley Sayre

illustrated by Steve Jenkins

The sun is rising.
Up, up.
It heats the air.
Up, up.

Wings stretch wide
to catch a ride
on **warming** air.
Going where?

Up, up!

Turkey vultures tilt, soar, scan
to **find** the **food** that vultures can...

...eat!

That snake **over** there?
No, no.

68

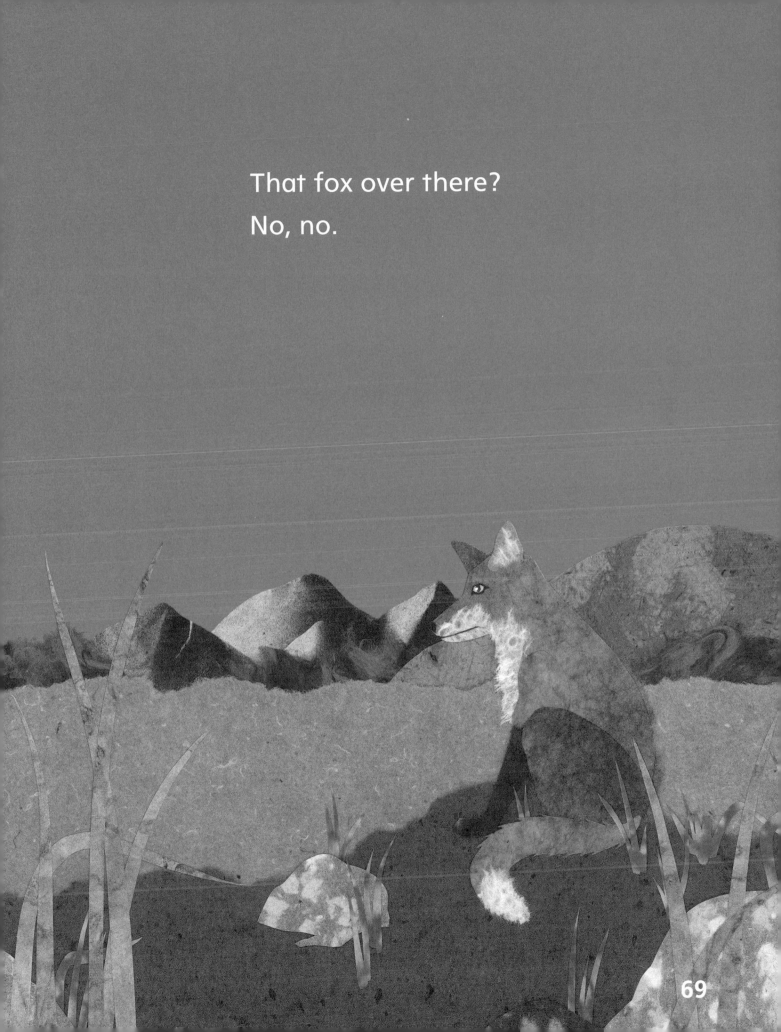

That fox over there?
No, no.

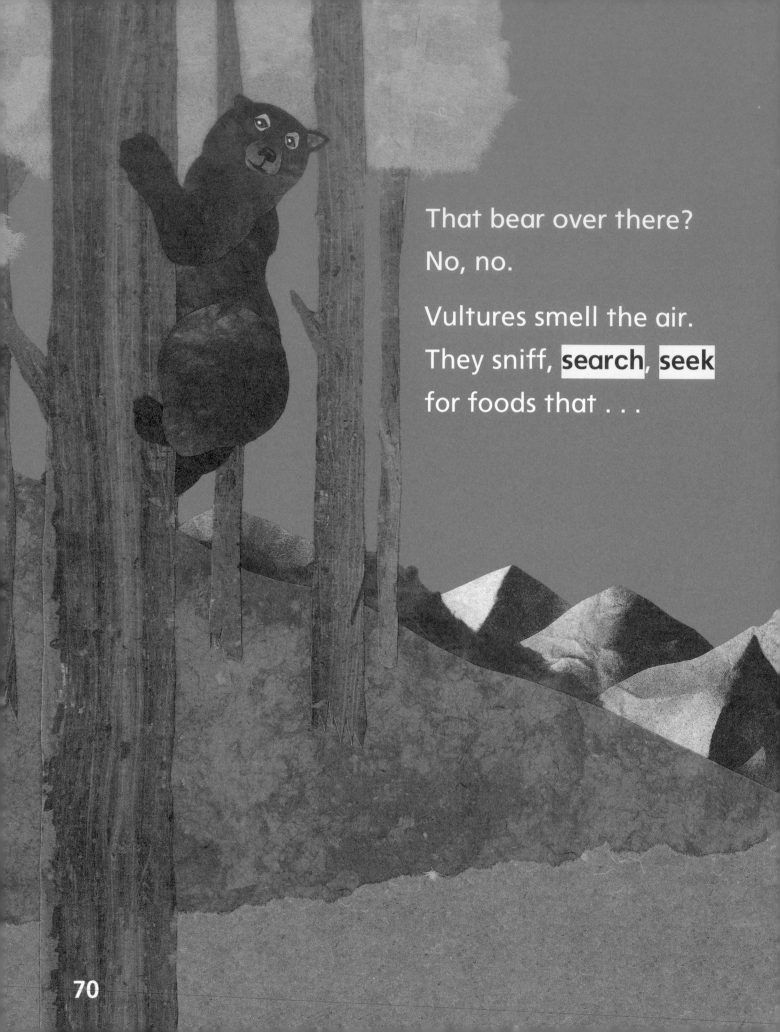

That bear over there?
No, no.

Vultures smell the air.
They sniff, **search**, **seek**
for foods that . . .

. . . REEK!

73

Those fragrant flowers?
No, no.

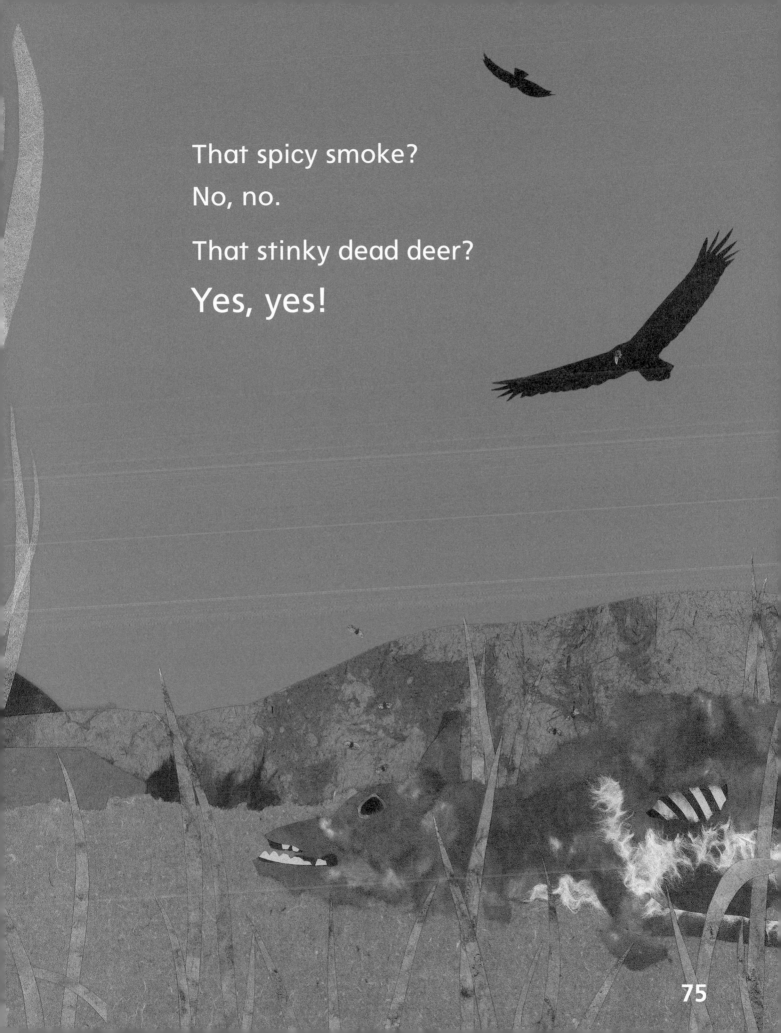

That spicy smoke?
No, no.

That stinky dead deer?
Yes, yes!

Vultures like a mess.
They land and dine.
Rotten is fine.

They eat, then clean.

Splash! Dry. Preen.

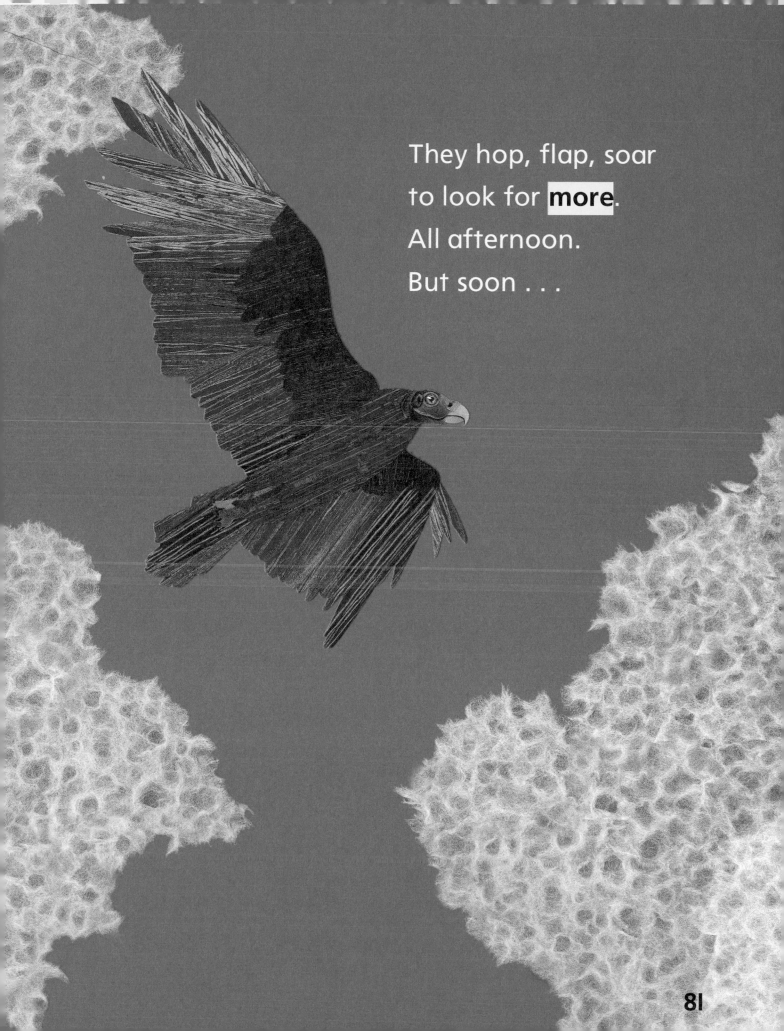

They hop, flap, soar
to look for **more**.
All afternoon.
But soon . . .

. . . the sun **starts** to sink.
Down, down.
The air starts to cool.
Down, down.
Wings glide, wings ride
through cooling air.

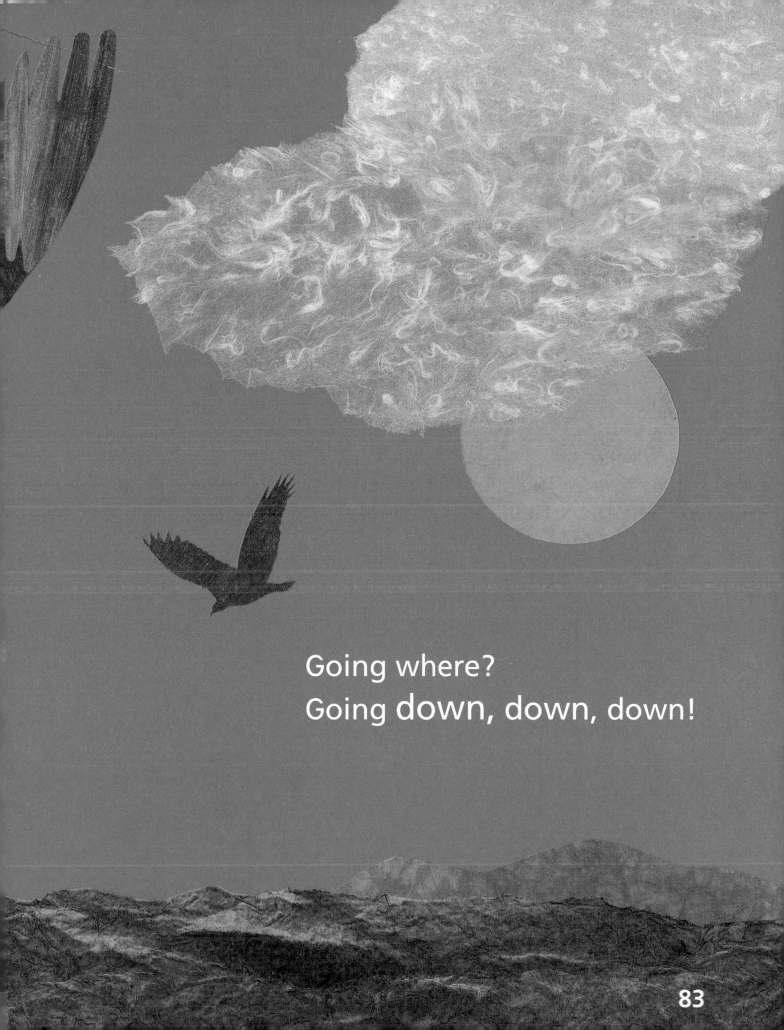

Going where?
Going down, down, down!

The vultures gather in vulture trees,
settle and sleep, like families.

Until . . .

. . . the morning sun rises.
Up, up.

It heats the air.
Up, up.

Wings stretch wide
to catch a ride
on warming air.
Going where?

Up, up!

Meet the Author

April Pulley Sayre loves science. She especially likes to come up with creative ways to tell stories about things in nature.

Meet the Illustrator

Steve Jenkins loves science, too. When he was growing up, he thought he would be a scientist, but he went to art school instead. Many of the books he illustrates are about animals.

Author's Purpose

April Pulley Sayre wanted to write about what a turkey vulture eats. Draw a picture of another bird eating. Write what the bird eats.

88

Respond to Reading

Retell

Use your own words to retell the main idea and important details in *Vulture View.*

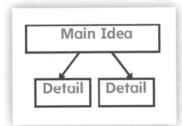

Text Evidence

1. What is *Vulture View* about?
   Main Idea and Details

2. Why didn't the turkey vulture eat the snake or the fox? **Main Idea and Details**

3. How can you tell that *Vulture View* is nonfiction? **Genre**

Make Connections

Think of a wild animal you know. What does it eat and how does it get its food? **Essential Question**

Compare Texts
Read about how a mouse survives winter.

When It's Snowing

by Aileen Fisher

Little Mouse, with narrow feet
that you keep so white and neat,
when it's snowing, freezing, blowing,
do you get enough to eat?

You're too little, Mouse, to stray
from your house on such a day.
Weren't you wise to gather scores
of munchy seeds to eat indoors!

Make Connections

? What does the little mouse do to survive?

Essential Question

Essential Question

What insects do you know? How are they alike and different?

Read about a fun pet who happens to be a fly.

Go Digital!

by Tedd Arnold

Chapter 1

A fly went flying.

He was looking for something to eat—

something tasty,

something slimy.

A boy went walking.

He was looking for
something to catch—
something smart,
something for
The Amazing Pet Show.

99

They met.

The boy **caught** the fly
in a jar.
"A pet!" he said.

The fly was mad.
He wanted to be free.
He stomped his foot
and said—

BUZZ!

The boy was surprised.
He said, "You **know** my name!
You are the smartest pet in
the world!"

Chapter 2

Buzz took the fly home.

"This is my pet," Buzz said
to Mom and Dad.

"He is smart. He can say my name. **Listen**!"

Buzz opened the jar.
The fly **flew** out.

"Flies can't be pets!" said
Dad. "They are pests!"
He got the fly swatter.
The fly cried—

BUZZ!

And Buzz came to the rescue.
"You are right," said Dad.
"This fly <u>is</u> smart!"

"He needs a name," said Mom.
Buzz thought for a minute.
"Fly Guy," said Buzz.
And Fly Guy said— BUZZ!

It was time for lunch.
Buzz gave Fly Guy
something to eat.

Fly Guy was happy.

Chapter 3

Buzz took Fly Guy to
The Amazing Pet Show.

The judges **laughed**.
"Flies can't be pets," they said.
"Flies are pests!"

Buzz was sad.
He opened the jar.
"Shoo, Fly Guy," he said.
"Flies can't be pets."

But Fly Guy liked Buzz.
He had an idea.
He did some **fancy** flying.

The judges **were** amazed. "The fly can do tricks," they said. "But flies can't be pets."

Then Fly Guy said—

The judges were more amazed. "The fly knows the boy's name," they said. "But flies can't be pets."

Fly Guy flew high, high, high
into the sky!

Then he dived down, down, down into the jar.

"The fly knows his jar!" the judges said. "This fly _is_ a pet!" So they let Fly Guy in the show.

He even won an award.

And so began a
beautiful friendship.

Meet Tedd Arnold

Tedd Arnold says, "My ideas come from different places at different times. A few years ago, it seemed like wherever I went with my family there was a pesky fly buzzing around us. Finally I decided to write a story about that little guy."

Author's Purpose

Tedd Arnold wanted to tell the story of an insect he knew about. Write about an insect you know. Draw a picture to go with your story.

Respond to Reading

Retell

Use your own words to retell *Hi! Fly Guy.*

Character	Clue	Point of View

Text Evidence

1. Who says, "You know my name!" to the fly? **Point of View**

2. Who thinks that flies are pests? **Point of View**

3. How can you tell that *Hi! Fly Guy* is a fantasy?
   Genre

Make Connections

How is Fly Guy like an insect you know? How is he different?
Essential Question

Compare Texts
Read about what insects can do.

Meet the Insects

We can find insects all around the globe. Insects can be lots of shapes, sizes, and colors. There are more insects than any other kind of animal.

How can you tell if a bug is an insect? Read on to find out.

The Body of an Insect

All insects have six legs and three **body** parts. Insects have no bones. The outside of an insect's body is hard. It **protects** the insect's body. Most insects have antennas and wings.

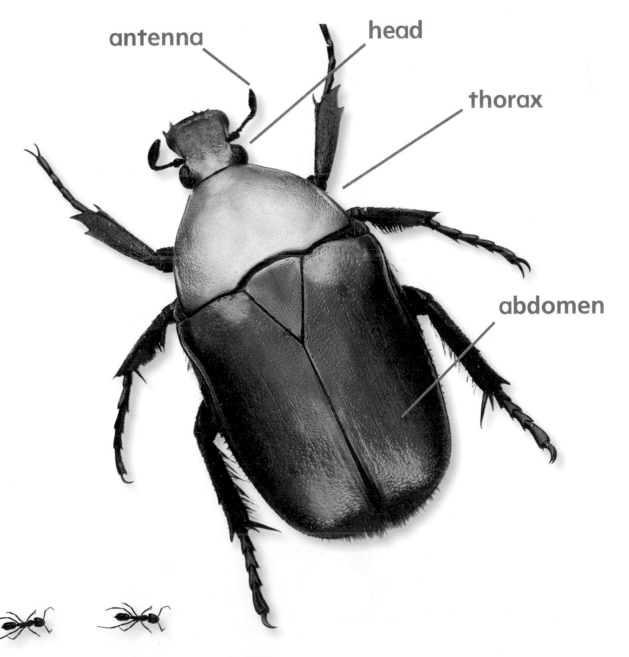

antenna

head

thorax

abdomen

Insect Senses

Insects use their **senses** to find food.
A fly smells with its antennas.
It tastes with its feet. That's
why flies like to land on food.

Insects do not see the same as we do.
Many insects have more than two eyes.
A grasshopper has five!

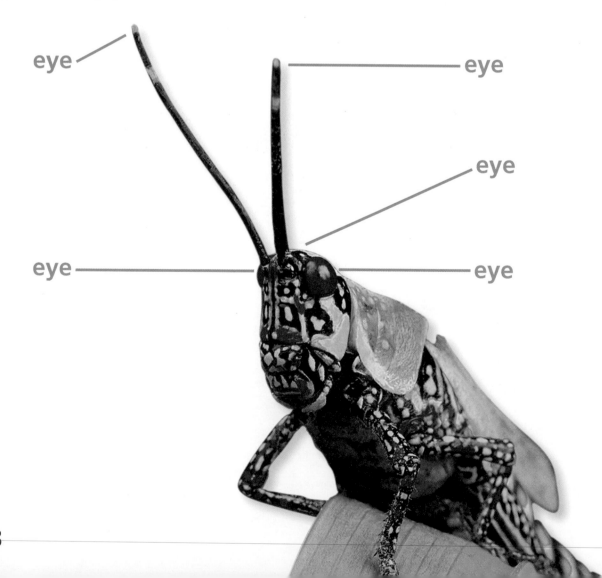

eye

eye

eye

eye

eye

Fun Insect Facts

Some ants can lift 30 times their own weight. This ant lifts a leaf.

A dragonfly can fly up to 60 miles an hour.

Termites build big mounds. They can be up to 30 feet high.

Insects are amazing!

Make Connections

What amazing thing could an ant do in a story? **Essential Question**

Essential Question

How do people work with animals?

Read about a gorilla who can do amazing things.

 Go Digital!

KOKO AND PENNY

What does a special teacher help Koko the gorilla to do?

Koko is a gorilla. Penny Patterson is a **woman**. But she is like Koko's mom.

Koko was very young when Penny began teaching her.

Penny **found** baby Koko at a zoo in 1972. Koko was a year old. Koko jumped into Penny's arms. She pulled her **near**. Penny liked Koko. She wanted to study her.

Penny wanted to teach Koko words. She showed her hand signs and **signals**. At first, Koko mostly asked for things she wanted. She **would** say words like "cookie" a lot!

This is how Koko says "sip".

This is how Koko says that she loves something.

This is how Koko says "toothbrush".

But soon Koko could say more. Now she knows over 1,000 words. When she is happy, Koko shows a smile. When she is sad, she points to her eyes. This means "cry". Koko is really **clever**!

Then Penny wanted to teach Koko how to do more things. She showed her how to use a pencil and paper. Koko works **hard**. She may be trying to **write** her name!

Koko likes to write notes and can sign her own name.

Koko is very gentle with her pets.

When Koko was 12, she would sign the word "cat" a lot. So Penny gave her a kitten. Koko was really kind to her kitty. She named him All Ball. She has had many more pets and has been kind to all of them.

These days Koko has lots of projects that keep her busy. She has a hobby. It is painting. Koko paints many things. Koko likes to name her paintings. She has done paintings named "Bird" and "Love".

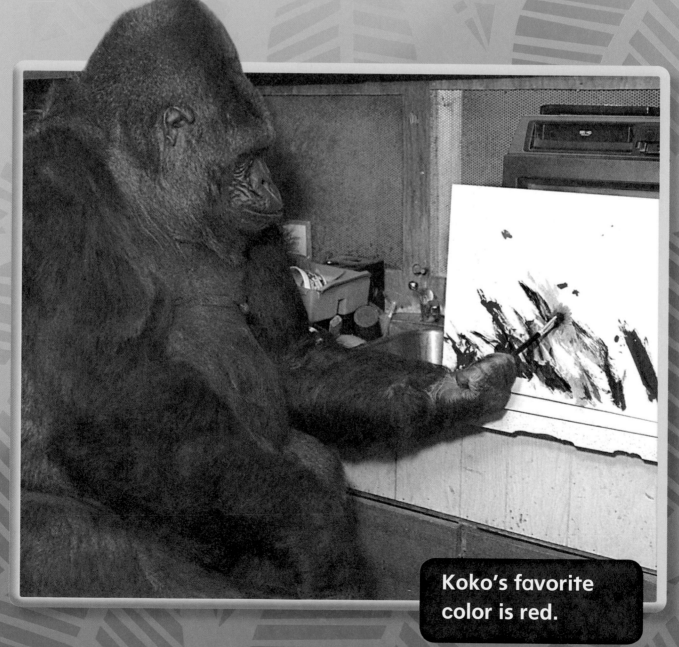

Ronald Cohn/The Gorilla Foundation/koko.org

Koko's favorite color is red.

Koko and Penny have worked and played together for a long time! Koko and Penny are quite a team.

Respond to Reading

1. What did Penny teach Koko to do first? **Sequence**

2. What did Koko learn after she began to use hand signals? **Sequence**

3. How do you know that *Koko and Penny* is nonfiction? **Genre**

4. What can you learn from studying animals? **Essential Question**

Compare Texts
Read about how a woman works to save gorillas.

SAVING MOUNTAIN GORILLAS

Gorillas make a new bed of plants each night.

Helen Gichohi lives in Kenya. She has a team that keeps gorillas like Koko safe.

People used to hunt gorillas. Then Helen and her team came. The team began to teach people not to hunt them. The team helps gorilla families stay together. They find the places where they sleep and help keep them safe. Soon we will have more gorillas. Safe families can grow big.

Dr. Helen Gichohi is President of the African Wildlife Foundation.

A ranger finds a gorilla. He takes notes. He will work to keep it safe.

Make Connections

How is Penny's job with Koko the same as Helen's job with the gorillas? How is it different? **Essential Question**

CCSS **Genre** Fantasy

Essential Question

How can we classify and categorize things?

Read about what happens when Toad loses his button.

Go Digital!

A Lost Button

from **Frog and Toad Are Friends**

by Arnold Lobel

Toad and Frog
went for a long walk.
They walked across
a **large** meadow.
They walked in the woods.
They walked along the river.
At last they went back home
to Toad's house.
"Oh, drat," said Toad.

"Not **only** do my feet hurt,
but I have lost
one of the buttons on my jacket."

"Don't worry," said Frog.
"We will go back
to all the places where we walked.
We will soon find your button."
They walked back to the large meadow.
They began to look for the button
in the tall grass.

"Here is your button!" cried Frog.

"That is not my button," said Toad.

"That button is black.

My button was white."

Toad **put** the black button
in his pocket.

A sparrow flew down.

"Excuse me," said the sparrow.

"Did you lose a button? I found one."

"That is not my button," said Toad.

"That button has two holes.

My button had **four** holes."

Toad put the button with two holes
in his pocket.

They went back to the woods
and looked on the dark paths.
"Here is your button," said Frog.
"That is not my button," cried Toad.
"That button is small.
My button was big."
Toad put the small button
in his pocket.

A raccoon came out from behind a tree.
"I heard that you were looking
for a button," he said.
"Here is one that I just found."
"That is not my button!" wailed Toad.
"That button is square.
My button was **round**."
Toad put the square button
in his pocket.

Frog and Toad went back to the river.

They looked for the button

in the mud.

"Here is your button," said Frog.

"That is not my button!" shouted Toad.

"That button is thin.

My button was thick."

Toad put the thin button
in his pocket. He was very angry.
He jumped up and down
and screamed,
"The **whole** world
is covered with buttons,
and not one of them is mine!"

Toad ran home and slammed the door.

There, on the floor,

he saw his white, four-holed,

big, round, thick button.

"Oh," said Toad.

"It was here all the time.

What a lot of **trouble**

I have made for Frog."

Toad took all of the buttons
out of his pocket.
He took his sewing box
down from the shelf.
Toad sewed the buttons
all over his jacket.

The next day Toad gave
his jacket to Frog.

Frog thought that it was beautiful.

He put it on and jumped for joy.

None of the buttons fell off.

Toad had sewed them on very well.

Meet Arnold Lobel

Arnold Lobel was often sick and missed many days of school when he was young. When he went back to school, he made friends by telling stories and drawing pictures.

Many years later, Lobel's children liked to catch frogs and toads. Lobel loved the animals and wrote about them in his Frog and Toad stories.

Author's Purpose

Arnold Lobel wanted to write about good friends. Write about your friend. Tell how you help each other.

Respond to Reading

Retell

Use your own words to retell "A Lost Button" from *Frog and Toad Are Friends*.

Character	Clue	Point of View

Text Evidence

1. How does Toad feel when he can't find his button? How do you know? **Point of View**

2. How does Frog feel when Toad gives him the jacket? **Point of View**

3. How can you tell that "A Lost Button" is a fantasy story? **Genre**

Make Connections

What are all the ways Toad describes his button?

Essential Question

Sort It Out

Some things are **alike**. Some are **different**. We can **sort** things by looking at what is the same about them. We can sort them by their size, shape, and color.

Find the buttons in this picture. Let's sort them!

How many round buttons can you see?
How many square buttons can you see?
What other shapes do you see?
Add up the number of red buttons.
Are there more red or yellow buttons?
Can you find buttons with four holes?
How else could you sort these buttons?

157

We can sort animals, too.
We can sort animals by features.
Which animals have four legs?
Which animals have two legs?
Which have none?
Which animals have patterns?
Which animals have yellow?
Which are bigger than you are?

We can classify animals by type.
Which are birds?
Which are reptiles?
Which are mammals?
What other types of
animals can you see?

Sorting is a lot of fun! Let's sort things in this scene. Think about what they have in common.

Which of these things have wheels?
Which eat food?
Which can fly?
Which have stripes?
Which have windows?
Which would you play with?

Illustration: Holli Conger

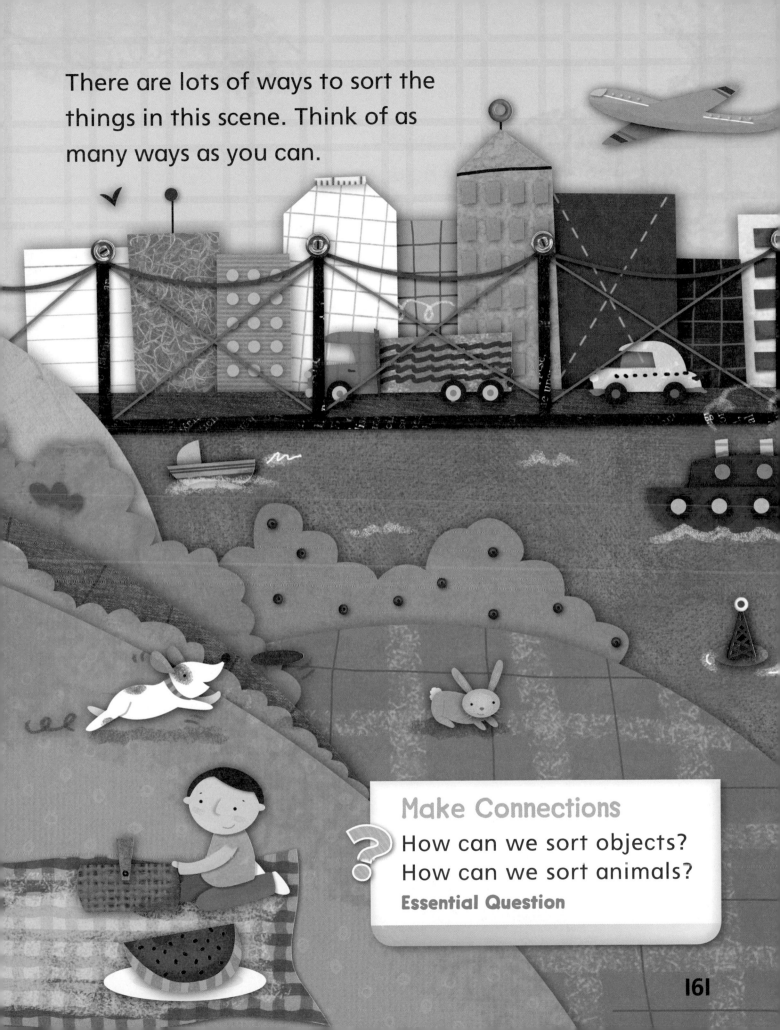

There are lots of ways to sort the things in this scene. Think of as many ways as you can.

Make Connections

How can we sort objects?
How can we sort animals?
Essential Question

161

Essential Question

What can you see in the sky?

Read about a kitten who thinks the moon is a bowl of milk.

Go Digital!

Kitten's First Full Moon

KEVIN HENKES

It was Kitten's first full moon.

When she saw it, she thought,

There's a little bowl of milk in the sky.

And she wanted it.

So she closed her eyes

and **stretched** her neck

and opened her mouth and licked.

But Kitten only ended up
with a bug on her tongue.
Poor Kitten!

Still, there was the little bowl

of milk, just waiting.

So she pulled herself together

and wiggled her bottom

and sprang from the top step of the porch.

But Kitten only tumbled—

bumping her nose and banging her ear

and pinching her tail.

Poor Kitten!

Still, there was the little bowl

of milk, just waiting.

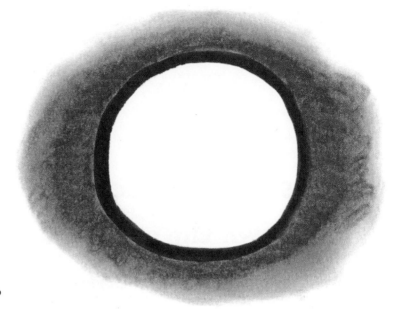

So she chased it—

down the sidewalk,

through the garden,

past the field,

and by the pond.

But Kitten never seemed to get

closer.

Poor Kitten!

Still, there was the little bowl

of milk, just waiting.

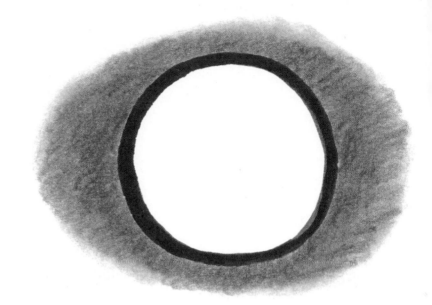

So she ran
to the tallest tree
she could find,
and she **climbed**
and climbed
and climbed
to the very top.

But Kitten
still couldn't reach
the bowl of milk,
and now she was
scared.
Poor Kitten!
What could she do?

Then, in the pond, Kitten saw
another bowl of milk.
And it was bigger.
What a night!

**So she raced down the tree
and raced through the grass**

and raced to the edge of the pond.

She leaped with all her might—

Poor Kitten!

She was wet and sad and tired and hungry.

So she went

back home—

and there was

a great big

bowl of milk

on the porch,

just waiting for her.

Lucky Kitten!

Meet Kevin Henkes

Kevin Henkes got the idea for *Kitten's First Full Moon* from a story he had begun to write many years before. Although he never finished this story, there was a line that read, "The cat thought the moon was a bowl of milk." He couldn't get this line out of his head, and slowly over the years the story of *Kitten's First Full Moon* formed.

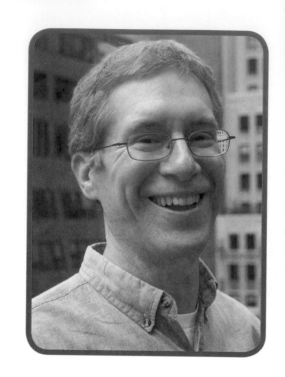

Author's Purpose

Kevin Henkes got his story idea from a line he liked. Can you think of a line from a rhyme or story that you like? Draw and write about it.

Respond to Reading

Retell

Use your own words to retell *Kitten's First Full Moon*.

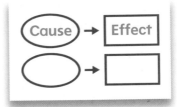

Text Evidence

1. What causes Kitten to chase the moon?
What causes Kitten to climb the tree?
Cause and Effect

2. What causes Kitten to jump into the pond?
Cause and Effect

3. How can you tell that *Kitten's First Full Moon* is a fantasy story? **Genre**

Make Connections

How is the moon like a bowl of milk? What else could the moon look like? **Essential Question**

Compare Texts
Read about something you see in the night sky.

THE MOON

The Night Sky

Think of what you see in the night sky. You see stars and the moon.

The moon is the neighbor closest to **Earth** in space. But it is very far away. The moon is about 250,000 miles from Earth!

The moon looks much smaller than it really is because it is so far away.

On some nights the moon looks bright and round. But it does not make its own light. Light from the sun shines on the moon. The light bounces back to Earth. We only see the lighted part of the moon that faces Earth.

The moon looks different every day of the month.

Why doesn't the moon look round every night?

The moon moves in a circle around the Earth.
As it circles, part of the moon faces the sun.

We see the part of the moon that is lighted.
That's why the moon seems to change shape.

We can see the moon better with a telescope.

People once thought the moon was made of cheese. They saw the face of a man in the moon.

Then **telescopes** helped us see the moon better. The telescopes showed hills and flat places. They showed craters, or big holes, too.

Then, in 1961, astronauts went to the moon. In 1969, other astronauts walked on it! They got a real close-up look.

Nothing grows on the moon. It is very rocky. Astronauts brought back moon rocks for us to see.

Maybe one day you will go to the moon, too!

Astronauts went into space and landed on the moon.

Make Connections

What kind of moon did Kitten in *Kitten's First Full Moon* see? Would she try to catch the moon every night? **Essential Question**

Genre Biography

Essential Question

What inventions do you know about?

Read about inventor, Thomas Edison.

Go Digital!

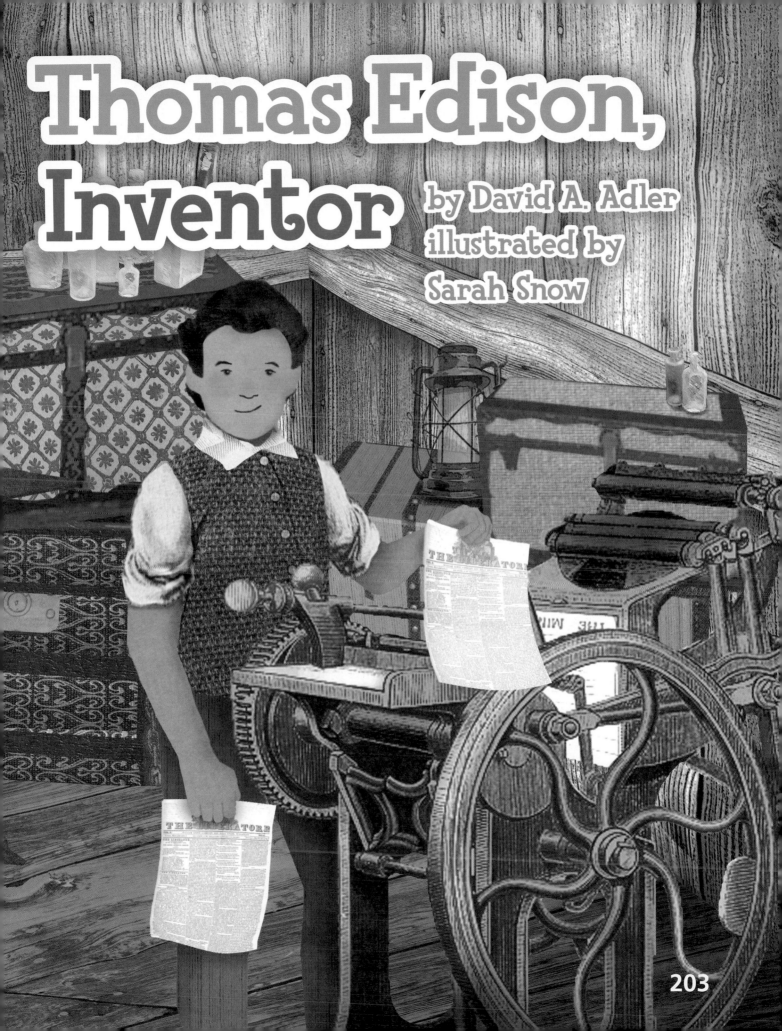

Thomas Edison, Inventor

by David A. Adler

illustrated by Sarah Snow

Young Tom Edison asked lots of questions. When someone told him, "I don't know," Tom had one more question. He asked, "Why don't you know?" He did lots of experiments to find out.

Tom watched a goose sit on some eggs. He saw the eggs hatch. He wanted to know what would happen if he sat on eggs.

So, Tom made a nest. Then, he put goose and chicken eggs in the nest. Next, he sat on the eggs and found out. Splat!

Young Tom also knew that birds ate worms and birds could fly. What if people ate worms? Tom **guessed** that they would fly, too.

So, he gave a girl a cup of chopped worms and water. The girl drank it and got sick. And she didn't fly.

Tom Edison, the boy who asked all those
questions and did those **unusual** experiments,
became the man whose inventions changed
the world.

Tom Edison was born in 1847 in Milan, Ohio. He was the seventh and youngest child of Sam and Nancy Edison.

Sam had a lumber mill. Nancy had been a teacher. When Tom had trouble in school, his mother became his teacher at home.

Chapter 2

Young Tom did many of his experiments in the cellar of his home. He had lots of jars of chemicals. He wanted to keep people from messing with them. To fix the problem, he had an **idea**. He wrote "poison" on each jar. He thought that would keep others away. He was **right**!

There were often smoke, strange smells, and loud noises in the Edison home. It all came from the cellar and from young Tom's experiments.

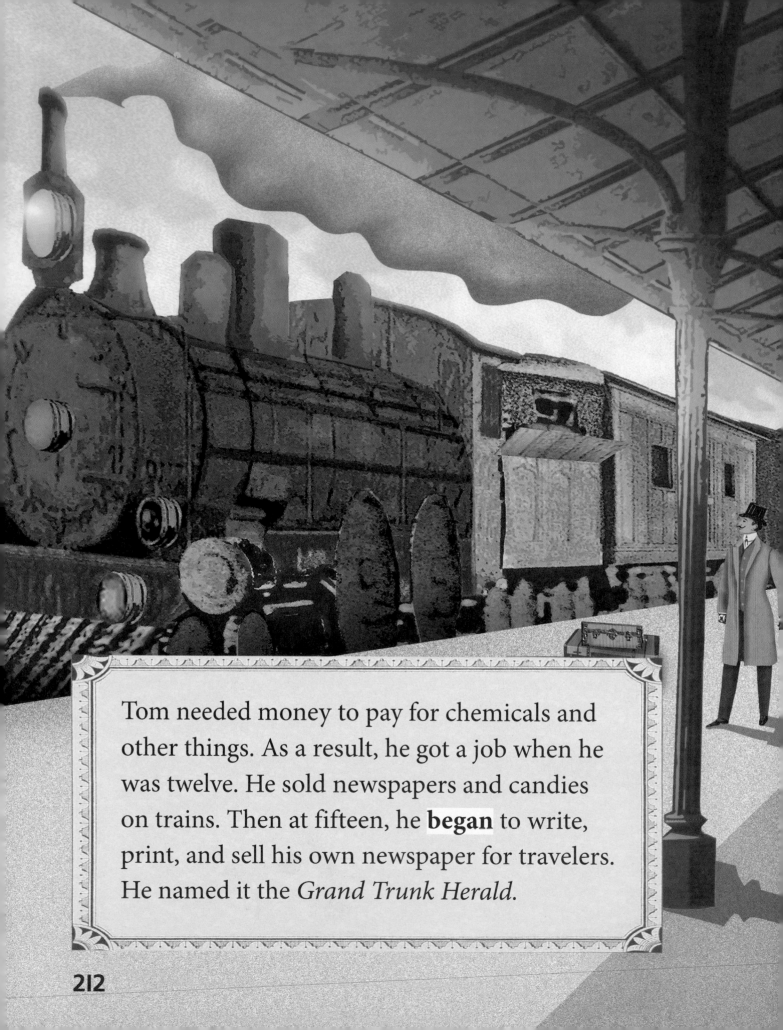

Tom needed money to pay for chemicals and other things. As a result, he got a job when he was twelve. He sold newspapers and candies on trains. Then at fifteen, he **began** to write, print, and sell his own newspaper for travelers. He named it the *Grand Trunk Herald*.

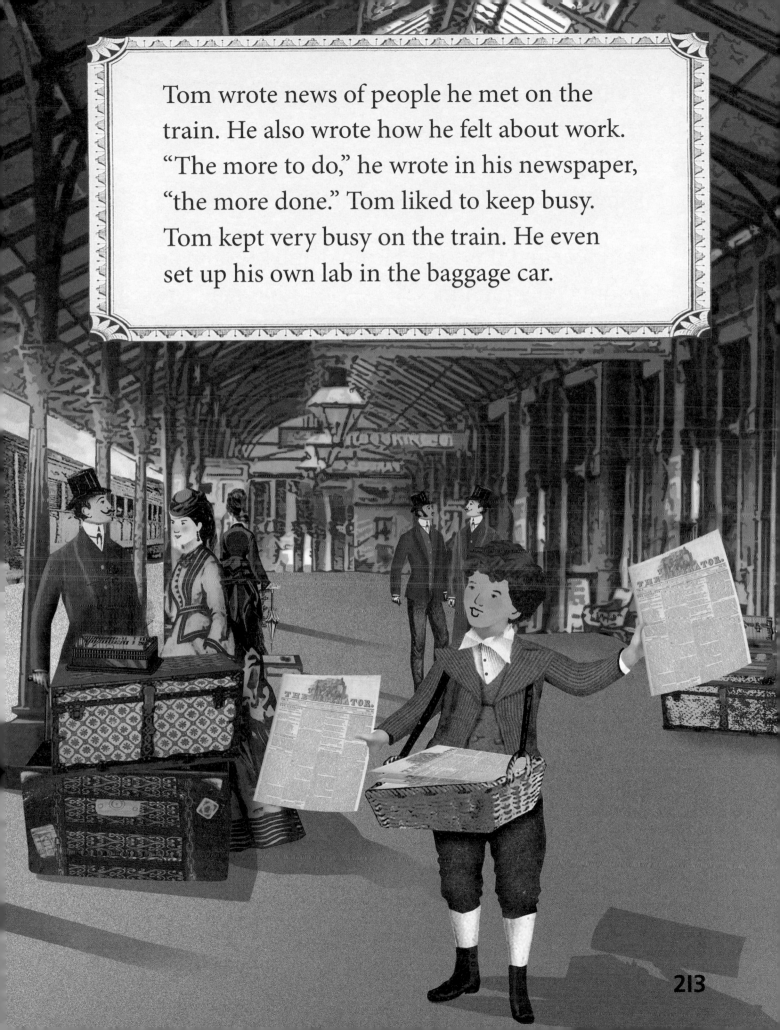

Tom wrote news of people he met on the train. He also wrote how he felt about work. "The more to do," he wrote in his newspaper, "the more done." Tom liked to keep busy. Tom kept very busy on the train. He even set up his own lab in the baggage car.

As Tom got older, he kept doing great things. There were no telephones at the time. Instead, messages were sent through telegraph wires. They were sent in a code of dots and dashes.

Tom **learned** the code. He got a job sending and reading telegraph messages. He found new ways to use the telegraph. Those were some of his first inventions.

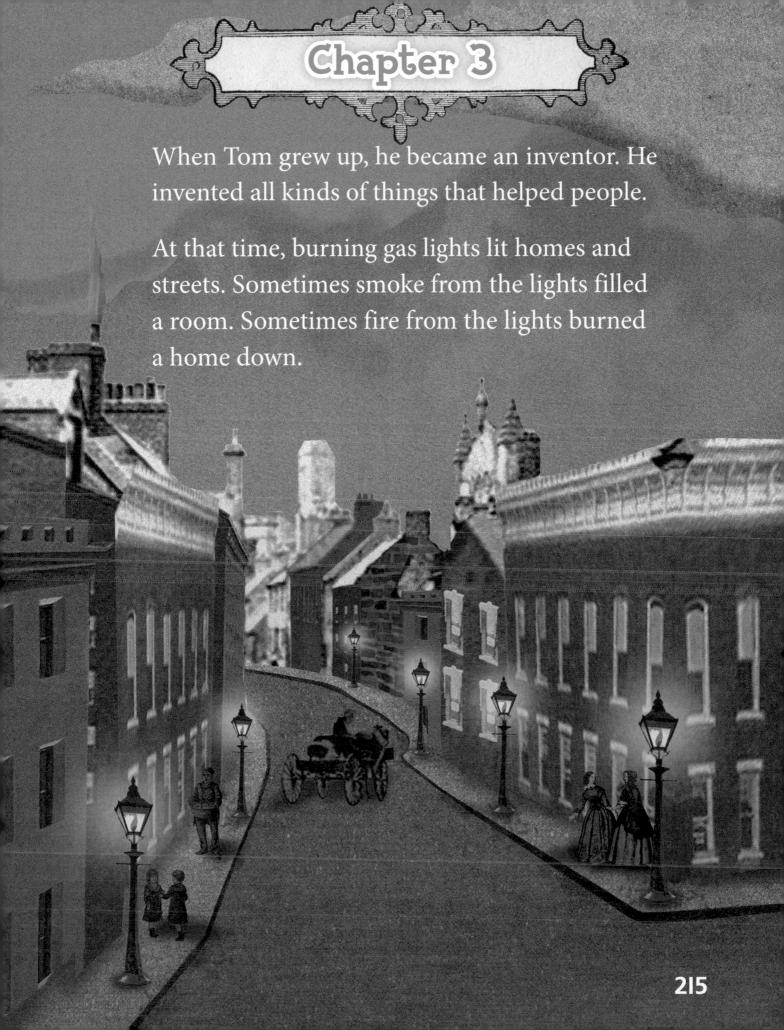

Chapter 3

When Tom grew up, he became an inventor. He invented all kinds of things that helped people.

At that time, burning gas lights lit homes and streets. Sometimes smoke from the lights filled a room. Sometimes fire from the lights burned a home down.

Tom was **sure** he could make a **better** light. So, he did experiments with electric light. He had lots of ideas. His notes filled hundreds of notebooks.

After more than a year of work, Tom did it. He made a light that was safe to use.

"The electric light is the light of the future," Tom said. "And it will be my light."

Edison's lights were big news. People came from all over to see them. Once they saw the Edison lights, they wanted them in their homes. Tom's lights brightened the world.

Tom Edison spent his whole life making great things. The things he made helped people everywhere.

Thomas Edison Photo Album

Thomas Alva Edison at age 15.

Edison invented the first machine that could record sounds and play them back. Without this, we might have no music players or movies and TV with sound today!

Edison made this early music player using his own sound machine.

Thomas Edison in his lab in Menlo Park, New Jersey.

Edison's lightbulb design looks similar to ones we use today.

Edison invented the first machine for viewing films. Without this machine, there would be no movies!

Meet the Author

David A. Adler says, "I love to write. With Tom Edison's invention, the light bulb, I can write even after the sun goes down."

David Adler has written all kinds of fiction and nonfiction for children. He especially likes writing biographies of people who acted in ways that children can learn from.

Author's Purpose

David A. Adler wanted to tell how curious Tom Edison was even when he was a boy. Think of something you are curious about. Write your question and how you could find the answer.

Respond to Reading

Retell

Use your own words to retell *Thomas Edison, Inventor*.

Problem

↓

Steps to Solution

↓

Solution

Text Evidence

1. What did young Tom do when he needed money to pay for chemicals? **Problem and Solution**

2. What was the problem with burning gas lights that lit homes and streets? How did Tom solve the problem? **Problem and Solution**

3. How can you tell that *Thomas Edison, Inventor* is a biography? **Genre**

Make Connections

How do electric lights make your life better? **Essential Question**

Compare Texts

Read about two inventions you know well.

Windshield Wipers

by Rebecca Kai Dotlich

Squish, squish,
squeegy-squish
tossing rain
side   to   side;
squish, squish,
squeegy-squish,
flap, flap,
puddle glide.
Slosh, slosh,
sloshing wash,
plish, plish,
tidal toss.
Squeegy-squish,
squish, squish, sway . . .

a perfect windshield
wiper day.

Scissors

by Rebecca Kai Dotlich

X slides open,
squeezes shut—
snip, snip, snip,
carve,
cut.

Illustration: Sarah Ackerley. Text: From *In the Spin of Things: Poetry in Motion* by Rebecca Kai Dotlich. Copyright © 2003 by Rebecca Kai Dotlich. Published by Wordsong, an imprint of Boyds Mills Press, Inc. Reprinted by Permission.

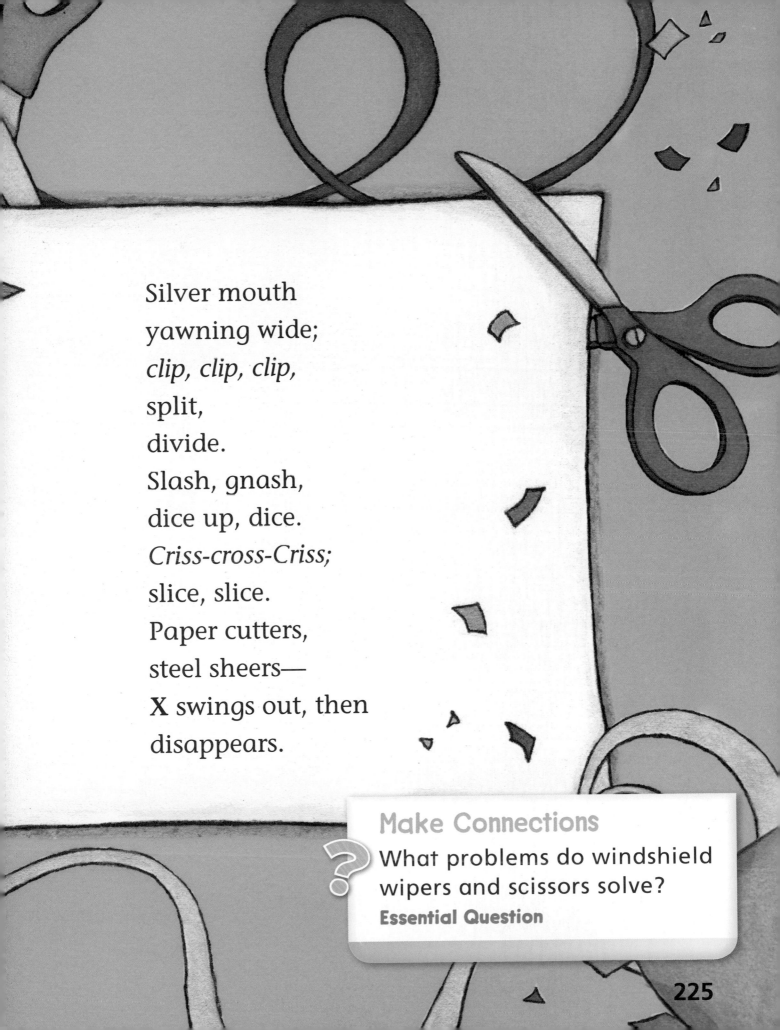

Silver mouth
yawning wide;
clip, clip, clip,
split,
divide.
Slash, gnash,
dice up, dice.
Criss-cross-Criss;
slice, slice.
Paper cutters,
steel sheers—
X swings out, then
disappears.

Make Connections

What problems do windshield wipers and scissors solve?

Essential Question

Genre Realistic Fiction

Essential Question

What sounds can you hear? How are they made?

Read about a boy who wants to whistle.

Go Digital!

Whistle
for
Willie

by Ezra Jack Keats

Oh, how Peter wished he could whistle!

He saw a boy playing with his dog. Whenever the boy whistled, the dog ran straight to him.

Peter tried and tried to whistle, but he couldn't.
So **instead** he began to turn himself around—
around and around he whirled …
faster and faster….

When he stopped
everything turned
down …
and up …

and up …
and down …
and around
and around.

Peter saw his dog, Willie, coming. Quick as a wink, he hid in an empty carton lying on the sidewalk.

"Wouldn't it be funny if I whistled?" Peter **thought**.
"Willie would stop and look all around to see
who it was."

Peter tried again to whistle—but still he couldn't.
So Willie just walked on.

Peter got out of the carton
and started home.
On the way he took some
colored chalks out of his pocket
and drew a long, long line
right up to his door.

He stood there and tried to whistle again.
He blew till his cheeks were tired.
But **nothing** happened.

He went into his house and put on his father's old hat to make himself feel more grown up. He looked into the mirror to practice whistling. Still no whistle!

When his mother saw what he was doing, Peter pretended that he was his father.

He said, "I've come home **early** today, dear. Is Peter here?"

His mother answered, "Why no, he's outside with Willie."

"Well, I'll go out and look for them," said Peter.

First he walked along a crack in the sidewalk. Then he tried to run away from his shadow.

He jumped off his shadow,
but when he landed they were
together again.

He came to the corner where the
carton was, and who should he
see but Willie!

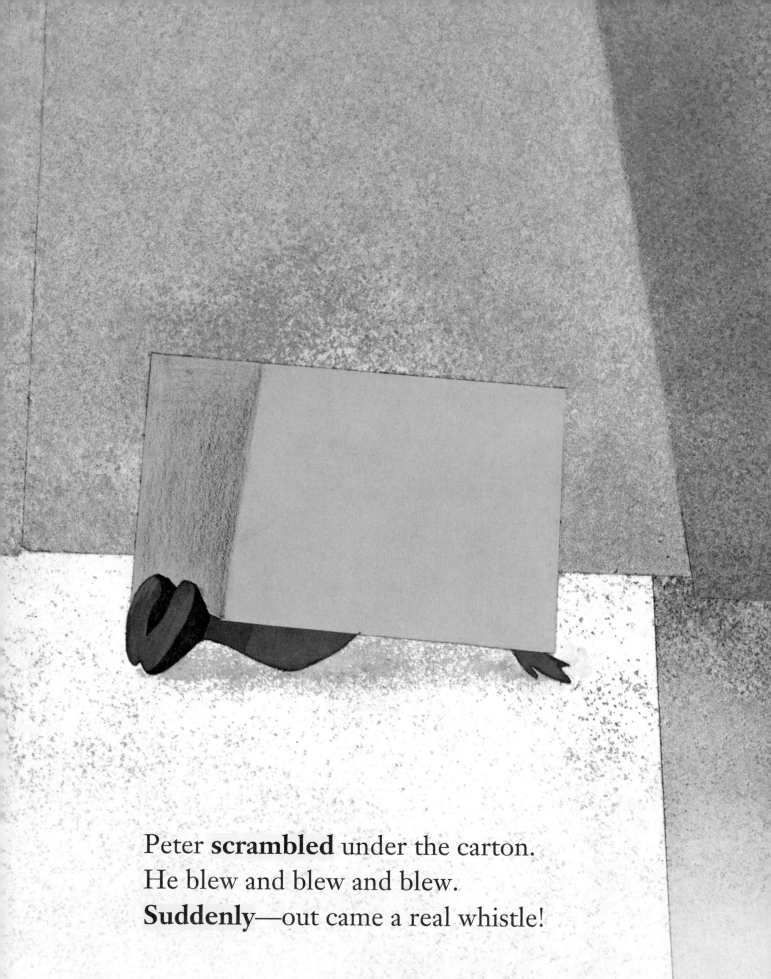

Peter **scrambled** under the carton.
He blew and blew and blew.
Suddenly—out came a real whistle!

Willie stopped and looked around to see
who it was.

"It's me," Peter shouted, and stood up.
Willie raced straight to him.

Peter ran home to show his father and mother what he could do. They loved Peter's whistling. So did Willie.

Peter's mother asked him and Willie to go
on an errand to the grocery store.

He whistled all the way there,
and he whistled all the way home.

Meet Ezra Jack Keats

Ezra Jack Keats sold his first painting when he was eight years old! When he grew up, he created many books for children. He used cut-out paper and a special type of paste to make the bright pictures. He won many awards for his work, but he was most pleased by letters from children who had read his books.

Author's Purpose
Ezra Jack Keats wanted to write about a boy who wished he could whistle. Write about something you wish you could do. Tell why you want to do it.

Respond to Reading

Retell

Use your own words to retell *Whistle for Willie*.

Problem
↓
Steps to Solution
↓
Solution

Text Evidence

1. What problem did Peter have?
Problem and Solution

2. How did Peter solve his problem?
Problem and Solution

3. How can you tell that *Whistle for Willie* is realistic fiction? **Genre**

Make Connections

What other sounds could Peter use to get Willie's attention?
Essential Question

Shake! Strike! Strum!

Shake, strike, strum! **Instruments** can be a lot of fun. Instruments make different kinds of sounds. Strike a drum. Rum-pum-pum. Strum a guitar. Plink, pling. Blow on a horn. Toot, toot. Shake it up!

Some sounds are nice to hear. Others are not. But all sounds have two things in common: pitch and volume.

Rubberball/Chris Alvanas/Getty Images

Pitch is how high or low a sound is. When you whistle for a dog, you make a high-pitched sound.

Volume is how loud or soft a sound is. When you whisper in class, you make a low-volume sound.

You can make fun sounds too. Make these instruments and start a band!

How to Make a Guitar

What You Need

- tissue box
- rubber bands
- tape
- ruler

What to Do

1. Stretch four to six rubber bands around the box.

2. Tape a ruler to the back. This is the guitar's neck.

3. Decorate the guitar.

4. Strum or pluck the rubber bands.

(t) Spike Mafford/Photodisc/Getty Images; (tc) Ursula Alter/Photographer's Choice RF/Getty Images; (bc) Stockdisc/PunchStock; (br) Stockdisc/PunchStock; (b) McGraw-Hill Companies Inc./Ken Cavanagh, Photographer

How to Make a Shaker

What You Need

- plastic bottle

- dried beans

- stickers

What to Do

1. Put beans into the bottle.

2. Put fun stickers on it.

3. Shake it and have fun.

Now you can shake, strike, strum, and have some fun!

Make Connections

How are sounds different? What sounds can you make? **Essential Question**

Essential Question

How do things get built?

Read about different kinds of bridges.

Go Digital!

Building Bridges

What kinds of bridges are there? How are they built?

1,125 feet

People **build** bridges to get from one point to another. Bridges go across water or land. They can be miles long or only a few feet.

Let's look at some of the world's most interesting bridges!

This bridge in France goes across a wide valley. It is the highest car bridge in the world.

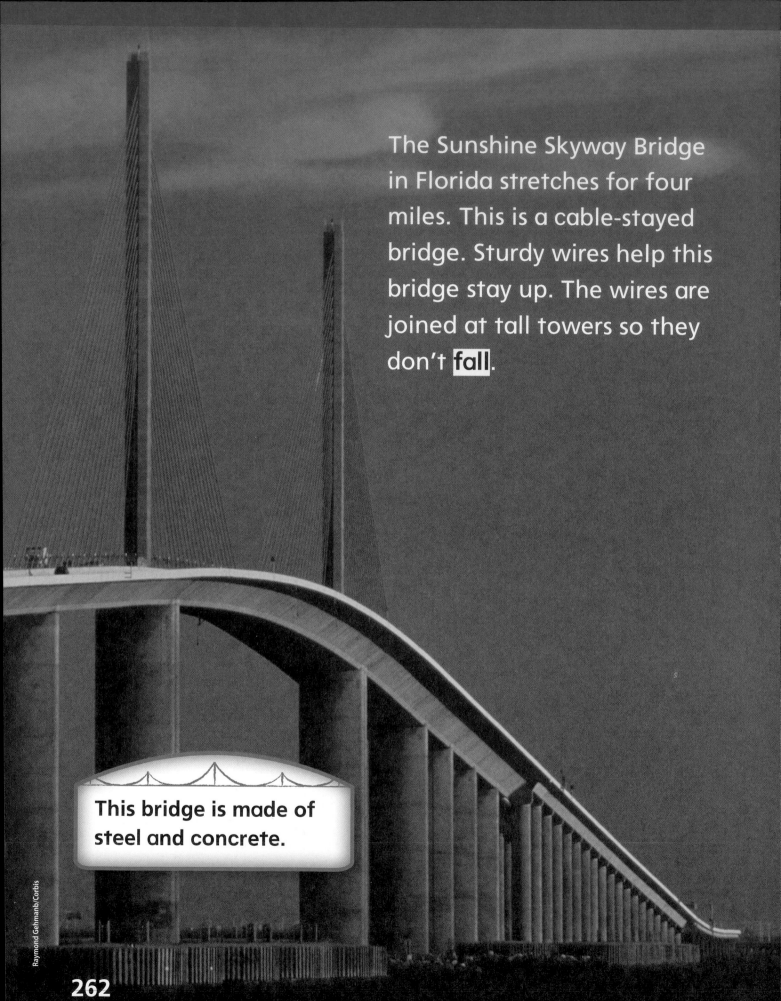

The Sunshine Skyway Bridge in Florida stretches for four miles. This is a cable-stayed bridge. Sturdy wires help this bridge stay up. The wires are joined at tall towers so they don't **fall**.

This bridge is made of steel and concrete.

Raymond Gehmanb/Corbis

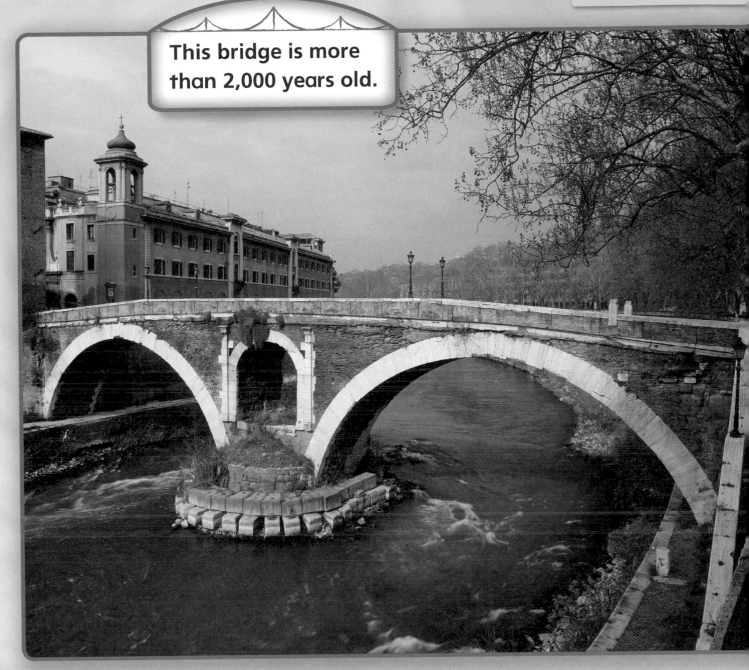

This bridge is more than 2,000 years old.

An arch bridge is like an upside-down U. This bridge has two big arches for boats to go though. The arches are the same size which helps **balance** the bridge. This bridge in Italy is made of brick, so it is really sturdy.

INTERFOTO/Alamy

263

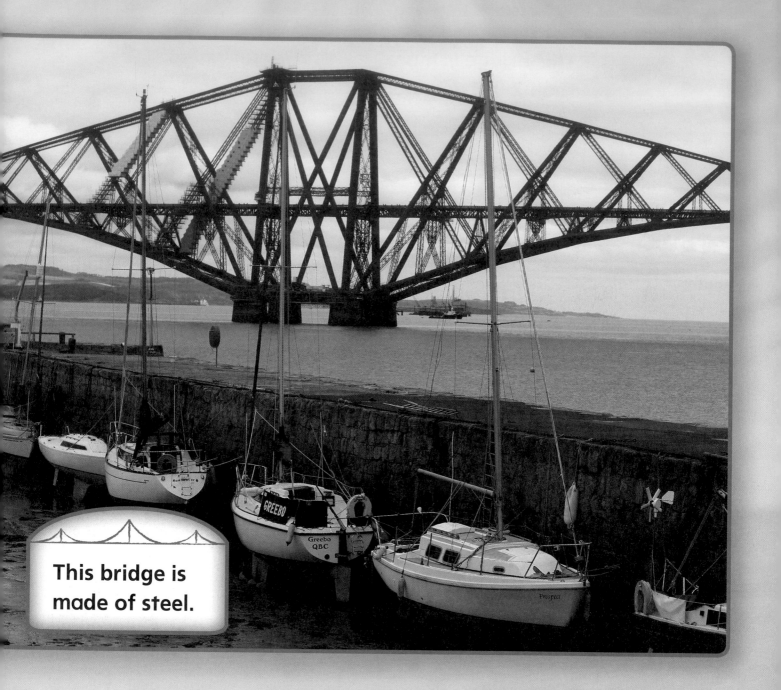

This bridge is made of steel.

The Firth of Forth Bridge in Scotland is a truss bridge. It is built **above** a river. Do you see the triangles? The roadway needs to be supported. The triangle tubes support it. The triangles join each **section** of the bridge.

Cars pay a toll, or **money**, to cross the Golden Gate Bridge in California. This suspension bridge has cables. The cables are supported by towers. Why is the bridge painted a bright color? The builders **knew** it must stand out in the fog. So they avoided colors like gray and painted it joyful orange.

The Golden Gate Bridge is a famous symbol of the United States.

Ed Pritchard/Stone/Getty Images

The bridge is flat so that people can cross.

Some bridges are one-of-a-kind. Rolling Bridge is in London, England. What happens when a boat comes **toward** the bridge? The bridge rises up and curls into a circle. Then the boat can pass.

There are many kinds of bridges. What kind of bridge can you think up?

Steve Speller/Alamy

When a boat passes the bridge begins to move.

Then the bridge becomes a circle.

Respond to Reading

1. What happens when a boat passes under the Rolling Bridge? **Cause and Effect**

2. Why is the Golden Gate Bridge painted orange? **Cause and Effect**

3. How do you know that *Building Bridges* is nonfiction? **Genre**

4. What is the same about how all bridges are built? **Essential Question**

Compare Texts
Read about a tiny building.

Small JOY

Tiny houses can go where their owners go!

Many people live in tiny houses. Tiny houses look small, but they feel big inside. This tiny house has one bedroom and one bathroom.

Dee Williams

268

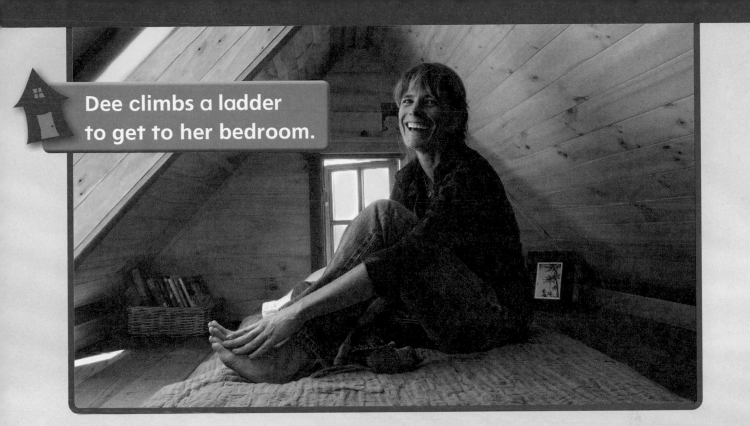

Dee climbs a ladder to get to her bedroom.

This tiny kitchen has everything Dee needs.

Tiny houses do not take a long time to build. Tiny houses do not cost a lot. And tiny houses do not take up a lot of energy or materials. They are good for the earth!

Make Connections

What would you have in your tiny house?
Essential Question

Essential Question

How can we work together to make our lives better?

Read about how some smart cows and hens get what they want.

 Go Digital!

270

Click, Clack, Moo
Cows That Type

by Doreen Cronin

illustrated by Betsy Lewin

Farmer Brown has a problem.
His cows like to type.
All day long he hears

Click, clack, **moo.**
Click, clack, **moo.**
Clickety, clack, **moo.**

At first, he couldn't believe his ears.
Cows that type.
Impossible!

Click, clack, **moo.**
Click, clack, **moo.**
Clickety, clack, **moo.**

Then, he couldn't believe his eyes.

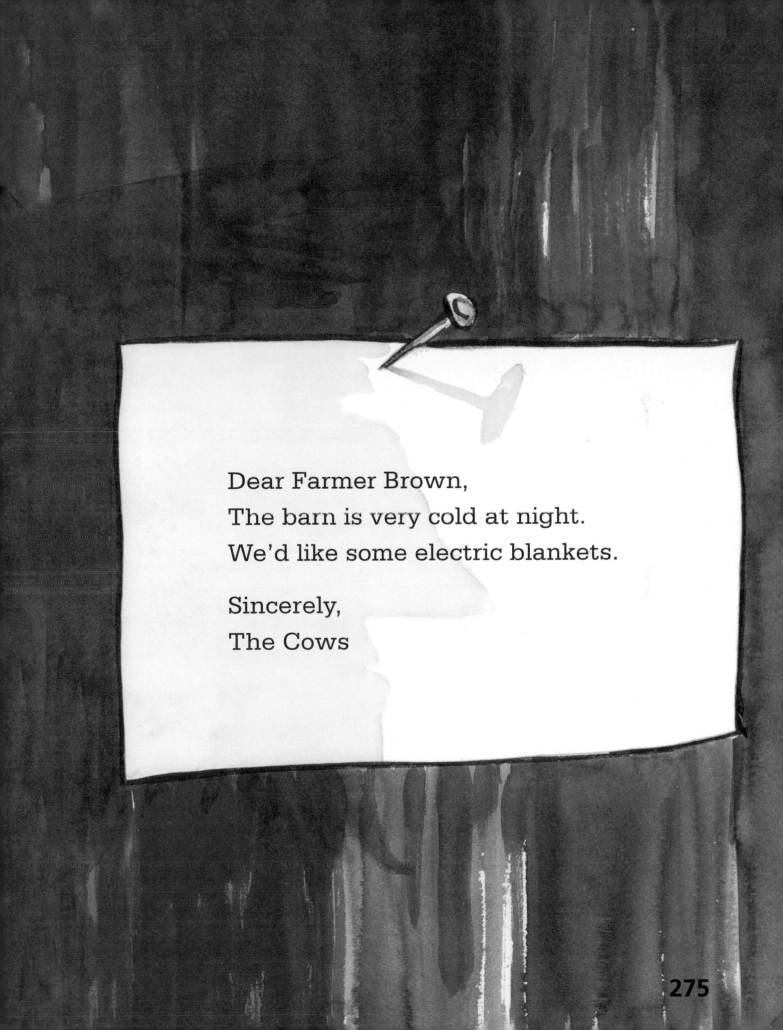

Dear Farmer Brown,
The barn is very cold at night.
We'd like some electric blankets.

Sincerely,
The Cows

It was bad **enough** the cows had found the old typewriter in the barn, now they wanted electric blankets! "No way," said Farmer Brown. "No electric blankets."

So the cows went on strike. They left a note on the barn **door**.

"No milk today!" cried Farmer Brown. In the background, he heard the cows busy at work:

Click, clack, **moo.**
Click, clack, **moo.**
Clickety, clack, **moo.**

The next day, he got another note:

Dear Farmer Brown,
The hens are cold too.
They'd like electric blankets.

Sincerely,
The Cows

The cows were growing impatient with the farmer. They left a new note on the barn door.

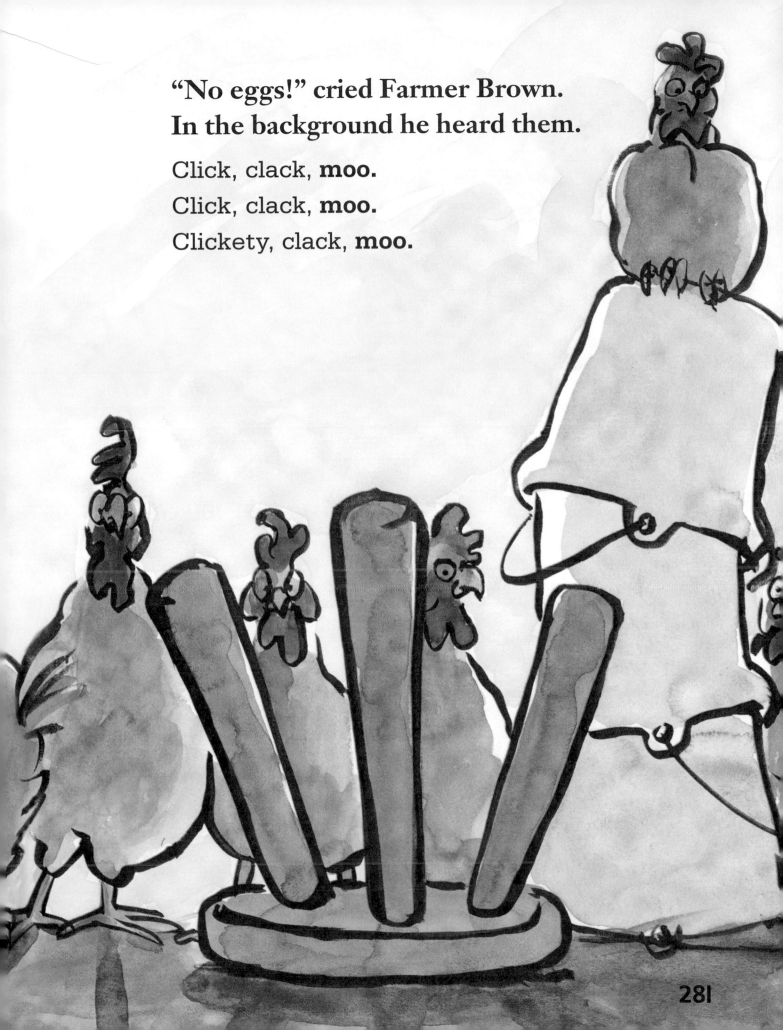

"No eggs!" cried Farmer Brown.
In the background he heard them.

Click, clack, **moo.**
Click, clack, **moo.**
Clickety, clack, **moo.**

"Cows that type. Hens on strike!
Whoever heard of such a thing?
How can I run a farm with no
milk and no eggs!" Farmer Brown
was furious.

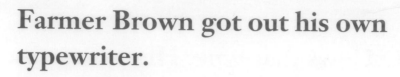

Farmer Brown got out his own
typewriter.

Dear Cows and Hens:
There will be no electric blankets.
You are cows and hens.
I **demand** milk and eggs.

Sincerely,
Farmer Brown

Duck was a neutral party, so he brought the ultimatum to the cows.

The cows held an **emergency**
meeting. All the animals gathered
around the barn to snoop, but none
of them could understand Moo.

All night long, Farmer Brown waited
for an **answer**.

287

Duck knocked on the door early
the next morning. He handed
Farmer Brown a note:

Dear Farmer Brown,
We will exchange our typewriter
for electric blankets.
Leave them outside the barn door
and we will send Duck over with
the typewriter.

Sincerely,
The Cows

Farmer Brown decided this was a good deal.

He left the blankets next to the barn door and waited for Duck to come with the typewriter.

The next morning he got a note:

Dear Farmer Brown,
The pond is quite boring.
We'd like a diving board.

Sincerely,
The Ducks

Click, clack, **quack.**
Click, clack, **quack.**
Clickety, clack, **quack.**

Meet the Author and Illustrator

Doreen

Betsy

Author **Doreen Cronin** and illustrator **Betsy Lewin** met for the first time after *Click, Clack, Moo: Cows That Type* was published.

Betsy says that she and Doreen have become good friends and enjoy working together. "Each of us is eager for the other's comments and advice."

Author's Purpose

Doreen Cronin and Betsy Lewin tell a story about how animals work together to get something they need. Write an idea for a story about kids who work together to get something they need.

Respond to Reading

Retell

Use your own words to retell *Click, Clack, Moo: Cows That Type*.

Text Evidence

1. How do the cows get Farmer Brown to do what they want? **Theme**

2. What message does the author want the reader to get? **Theme**

3. How can you tell that *Click, Clack, Moo: Cows That Type* is a fantasy? **Genre**

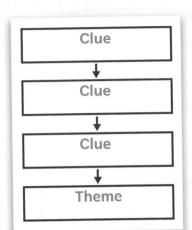

Clue
↓

Clue
↓

Clue
↓

Theme

Make Connections

What kind of deal might the ducks make with Farmer Brown?

Essential Question

295

Compare Texts
Read about how people made their lives better.

100 years ago only men could vote.

March on!

How can people make their lives better? One way is to work together.

One hundred years ago, women in America were not allowed to vote. That meant they could not pick their leaders or help decide on laws and rules.

Many women and men did not think this was fair. So they got together to **protest**. They marched and made speeches. They carried picket signs. People listened. In 1920, women got the **right** to vote.

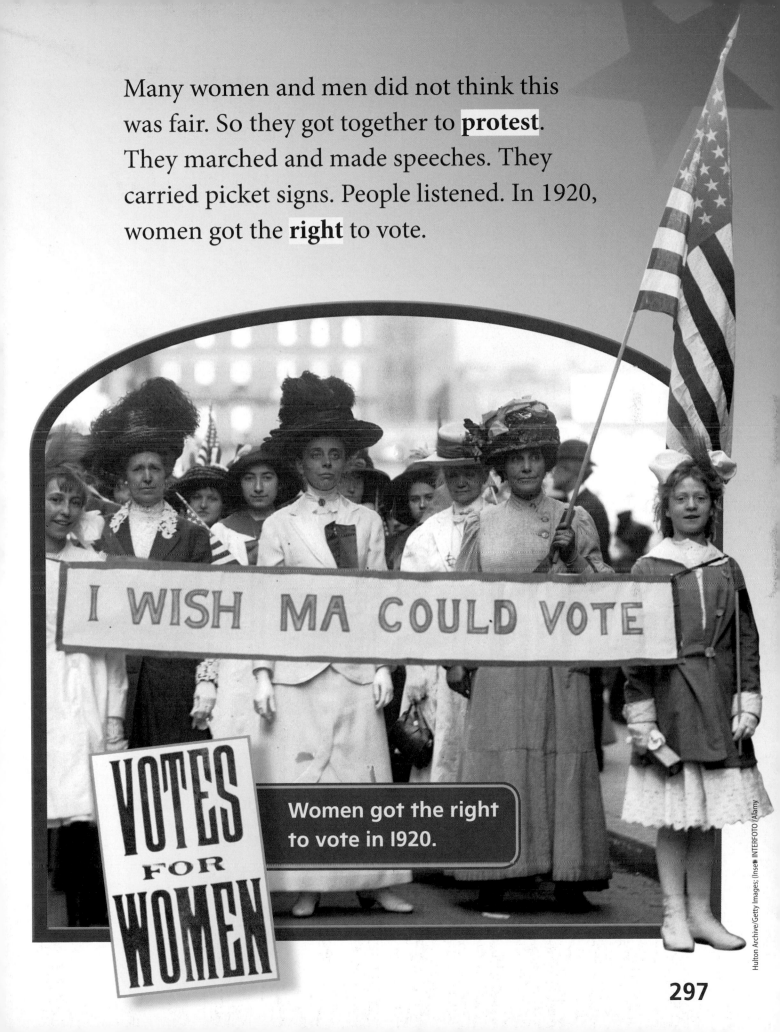

I WISH MA COULD VOTE

VOTES FOR WOMEN

Women got the right to vote in 1920.

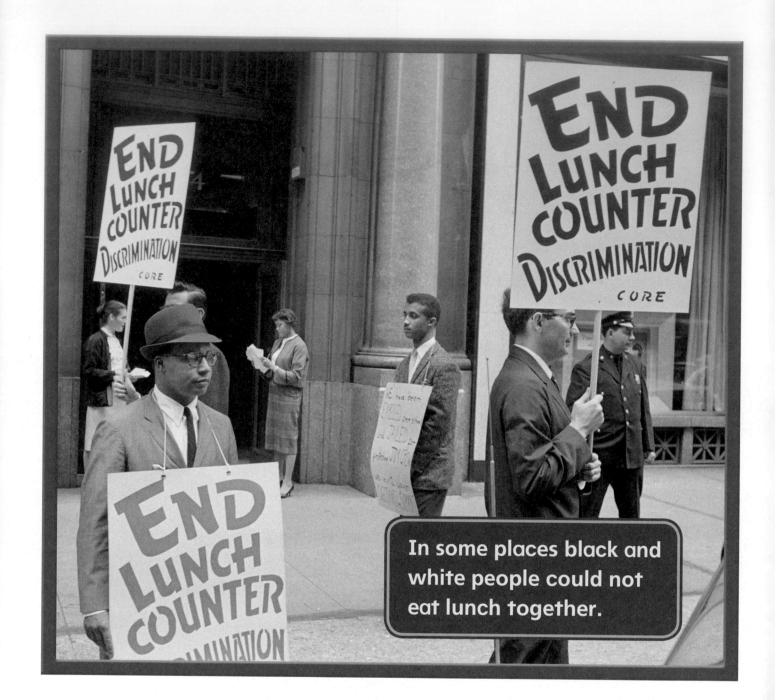

In some places black and white people could not eat lunch together.

For many years, black people in our country did not have the same rights as other people. Some jobs would not hire black people. Some stores would not let black people shop, and some schools would not let black children in.

Many people did not think this was fair. So they got together and marched. Leaders like Martin Luther King, Jr. made speeches. He said all people should have the same rights.

People listened. Laws were passed that said all people must be treated equally.

People from all over came to support equal rights.

In the 1960s people all over the country got together to help farm workers. Many of these workers came to this country to pick crops. But they did not get much money. They did not have good places to live or schools for their children.

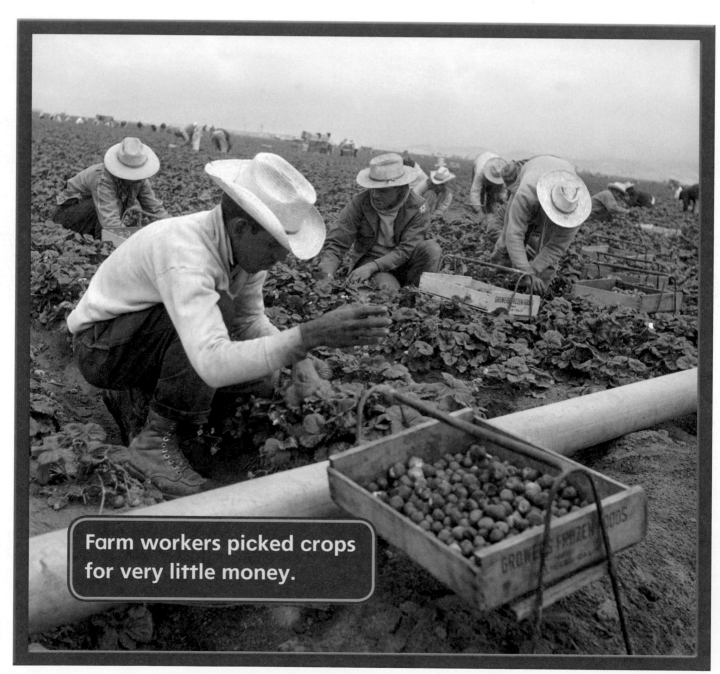

Farm workers picked crops for very little money.

People worked together to change this. Leaders like César Chávez organized the workers. People all over the country marched with them. The farmers listened. They gave the workers more pay and better homes. It is possible to **improve** our lives if we work together!

Make Connections

How are the animals in *Click, Clack, Moo: Cows That Type* like the people in "March On!"?
Essential Question

César Chávez organized farm workers to fight for better lives.

Essential Question
Who helps you?
Read about a girl who is a lot like you!

Go Digital!

Meet * Rosina

* Rosina

by George Ancona

(bl) The McGraw-Hill Companies, Inc; (br) Stockbyte/PunchStock.

Hi!

I'm

Rosina

I am deaf, so I talk with my hands.

I go to a special school for deaf children. All of our teachers teach with American Sign Language. We call this signing.

We study math, writing, reading, and art. It's the same as in other schools.

My **brother** Emilio also goes to my
school. We play basketball during
recess.

My **mother** and aunt are deaf, too. They both work at my school. Mom is a teacher's helper.

My Aunt Carla shows us **pictures** of students who used to go to the school. My mom was one of them. My aunt **often** tells stories about when my parents were young.

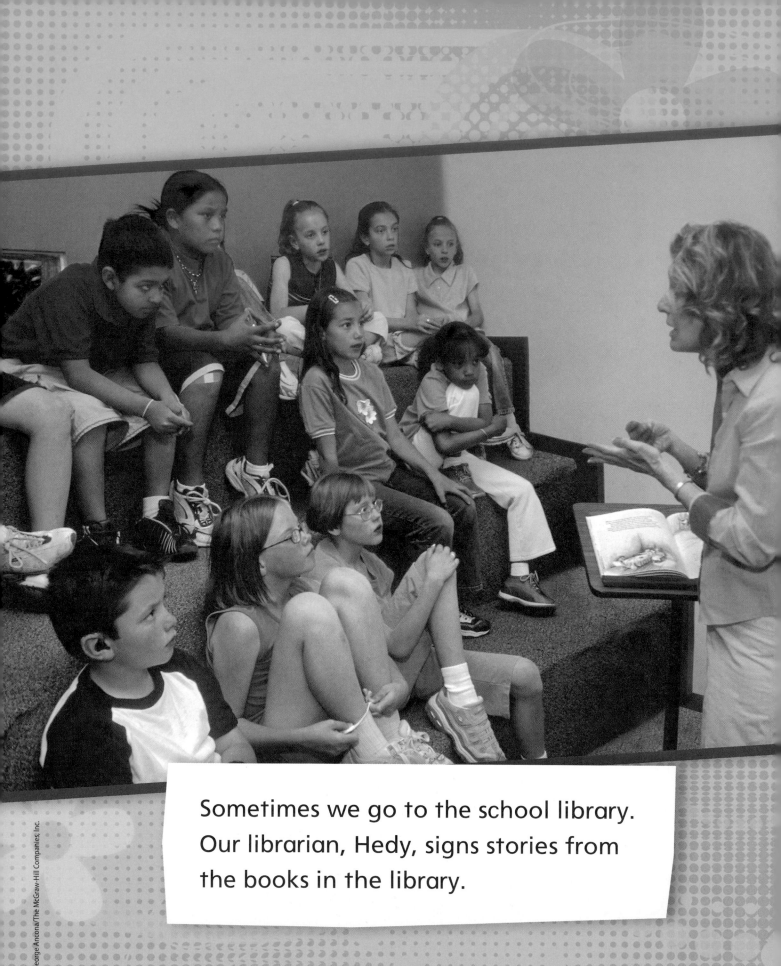

Sometimes we go to the school library. Our librarian, Hedy, signs stories from the books in the library.

Hedy is good at telling stories. She makes us feel as if we're in the story. The story can make us feel sad, scared, worried, or happy.

I **love** going to art class. I like to paint. Here I am painting a picture of myself!

Our class made up a story. It is about a deaf **father** who woke up one day with four arms. We wrote it and did all the drawings. Then we made it into a book called *Too Many Hands.*

I like sports. We are playing rugby. The way we play is to tag the person carrying the ball. Then he or she throws it to another player on the team. By running fast we can get away and cross the goal line.

Our team played other schools. We beat all of the other teams and **accepted** a big trophy.

We were so happy! We splashed our coach in water. Some of us got wet, too. We are all **friends** so no one got mad.

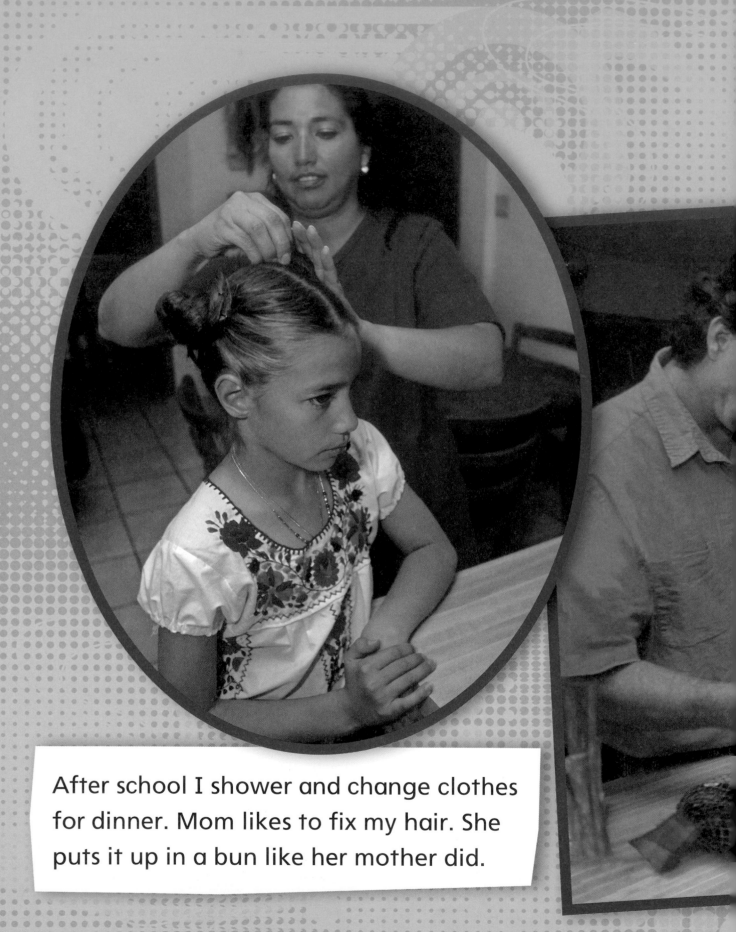

After school I shower and change clothes for dinner. Mom likes to fix my hair. She puts it up in a bun like her mother did.

At home we all help Mom cook meals.
I chop lettuce. Emilio cuts up cheese.
Dad makes guacamole.

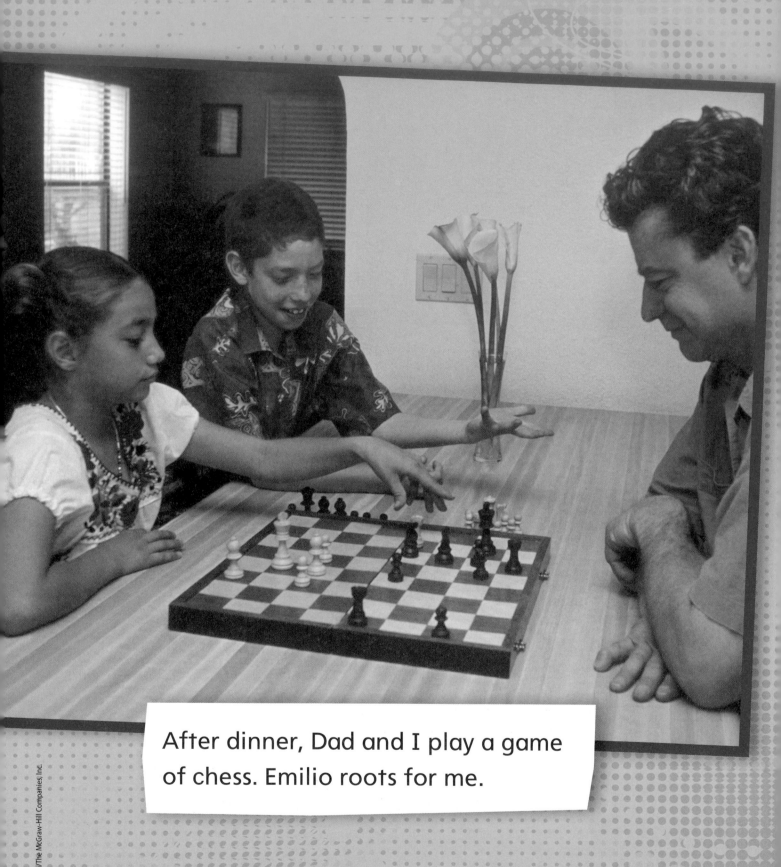

After dinner, Dad and I play a game of chess. Emilio roots for me.

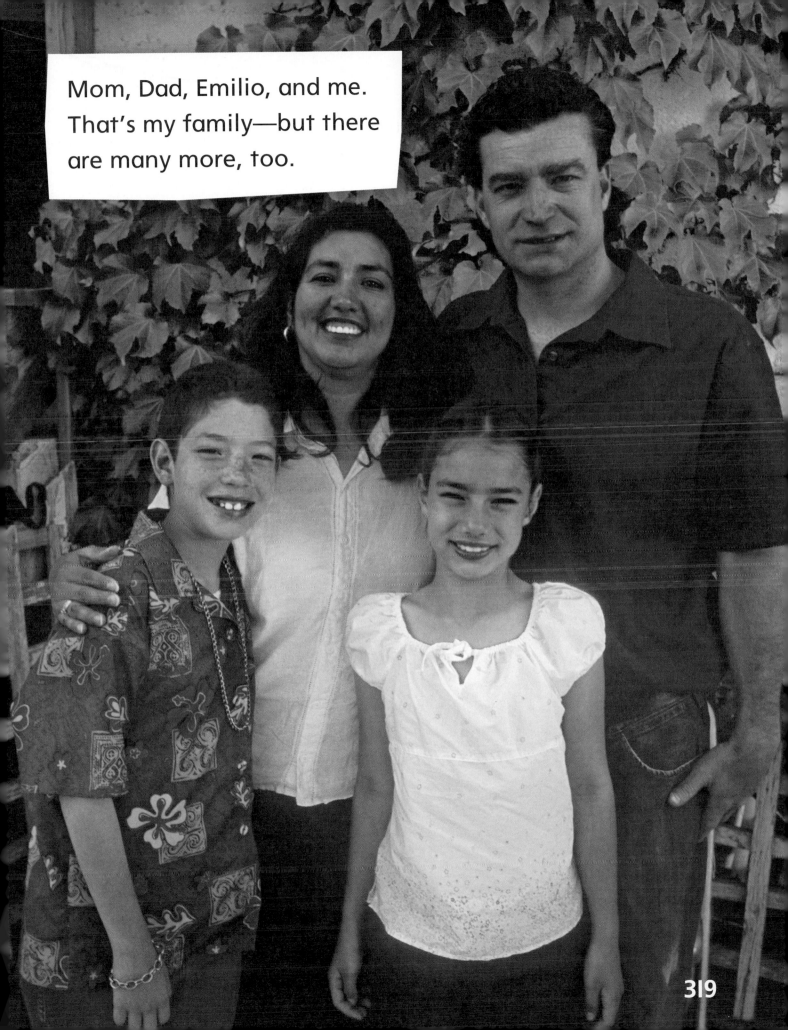

Mom, Dad, Emilio, and me. That's my family—but there are many more, too.

We are a big family. I have lots of aunts, cousins, grandpas, and grandmas. Most of my mom's family is deaf. My whole family uses sign language to talk to each other.

This is how we sign "goodbye."

Meet George Ancona

George Ancona wrote the words and took the photographs for this piece. He learned how to take photographs from his father when he was growing up. His father developed pictures in their bathroom!

Today, George likes to photograph people in their everyday lives. Before George wrote this book, he already knew some sign language. In this picture, he is signing, "I love you!"

Author's Purpose

George Ancona shows how Rosina spends a day. Write a journal entry about what you did yesterday.

George Ancona

Respond to Reading

Retell

Use your own words to retell *Meet Rosina*.

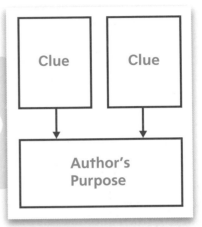

Text Evidence

1. How is Rosina like you? How is she different? **Author's Purpose**

2. Why do you think the author wrote this book? Why do you think he illustrated it with photographs? **Author's Purpose**

3. How can you tell that *Meet Rosina* is nonfiction? **Genre**

Make Connections

How does Rosina's family help her? Who else helps her? **Essential Question**

Compare Texts

Read about a grandmother who helps in her own special way.

Abuelita's Lap

by Pat Mora

I know a place where I can sit
and tell about my day,
tell every color that I saw
from green to cactus gray.

I know a place where I can sit
and hear a favorite beat,
her heart and *cuentos* from the past,
the rhythms honey-sweet.

I know a place where I can sit
and listen to a star,
listen to its silent song
gliding from afar.

I know a place where I can sit
and hear the wind go by,
hearing it spinning round my house,
my whirling lullaby.

Make Connections

 How does the boy feel about his grandmother?
Essential Question

Genre Realistic Fiction

Essential Question

How can weather affect us?

Read about why a school has to be rebuilt every year.

Go Digital!

Rain School

by James Rumford

In the **country** of Chad, it is the first day of school. The dry dirt road is filling up with **children**.

Big brothers and big sisters are leading the way.

"Will they give us a notebook?" Thomas asks.

"Will they give us a pencil?"

"Will I learn to read like you?"

"Stop asking so many **questions** and keep up," say the big brothers and big sisters.

Thomas arrives at the schoolyard,
but there are no classrooms.

There are no desks.

It doesn't matter.

There is a teacher.

"We will build our school,"
she says. "This is the first lesson."

Thomas learns to make mud bricks
and dry them in the sun.

He learns to build mud walls and mud desks.

He **gathers** grass and saplings with the other children, and they make a roof.

Inside it is cool. It smells of the earth. It smells of the fields ready for planting.

Thomas helps bring in little wooden stools.

Everyone sits down.

This is the moment they have **been** waiting for.

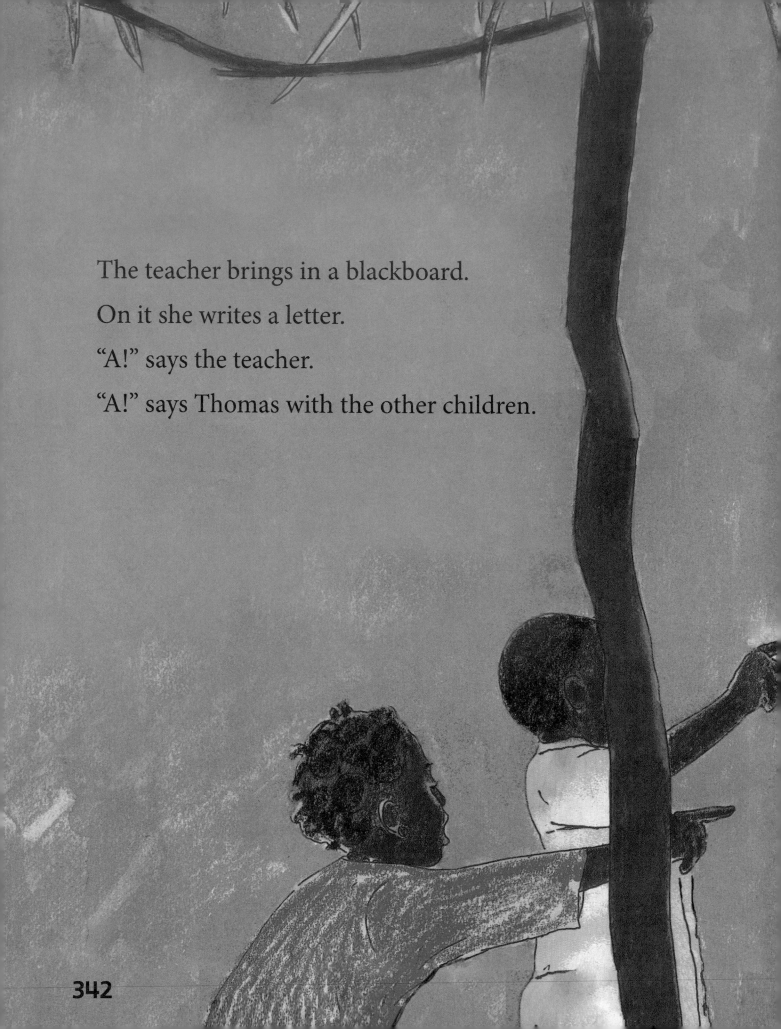

The teacher brings in a blackboard.

On it she writes a letter.

"A!" says the teacher.

"A!" says Thomas with the other children.

The teacher writes the letter with big strokes in the air.

The students do the same, over and over.

"Wonderful," says the teacher.

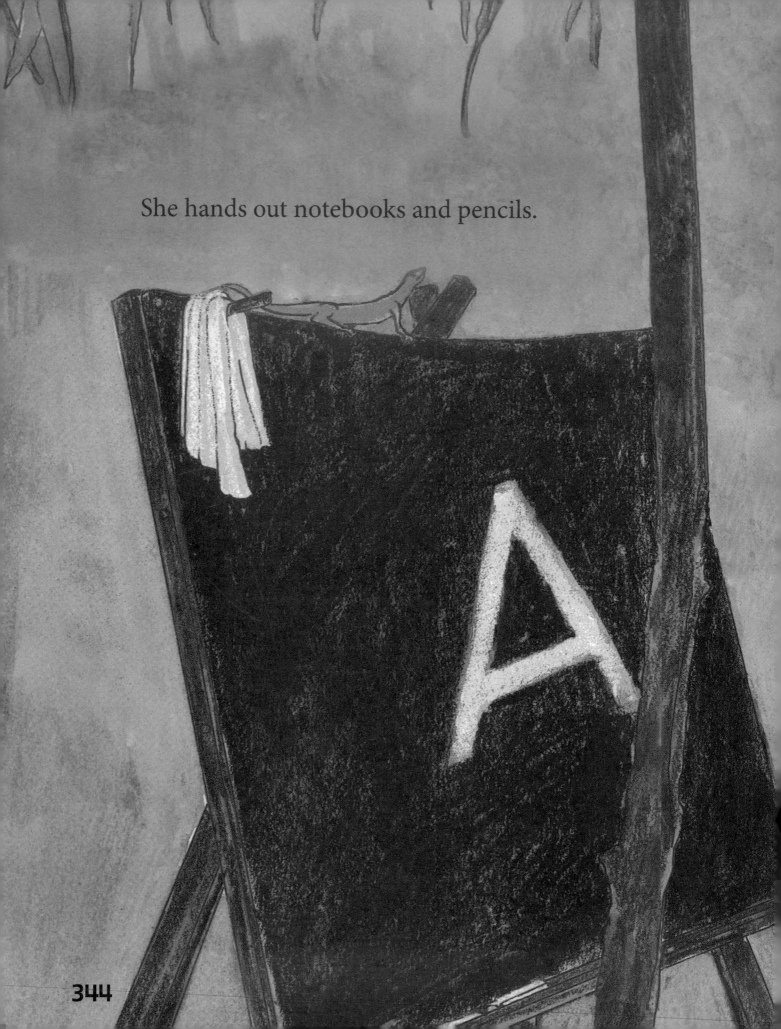

She hands out notebooks and pencils.

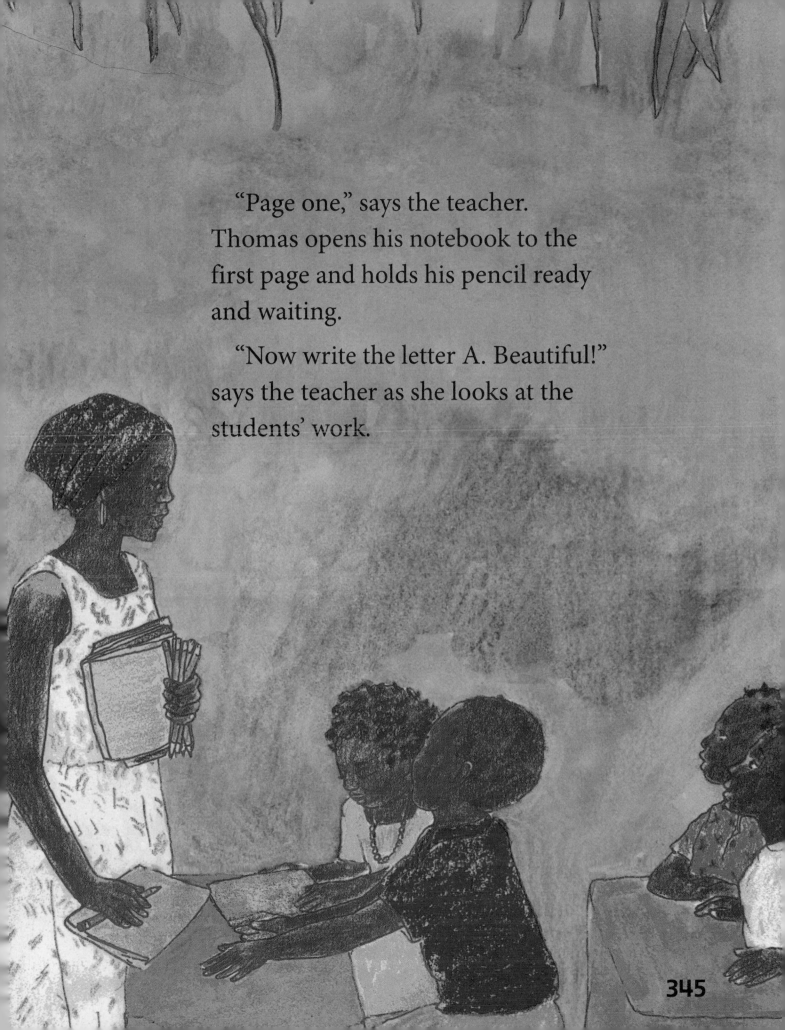

"Page one," says the teacher.
Thomas opens his notebook to the
first page and holds his pencil ready
and waiting.

"Now write the letter A. Beautiful!"
says the teacher as she looks at the
students' work.

Every day Thomas learns something new.

Every day the teacher cheers him and the other children on. "Excellent job," she says. "Perfect, my learning friends!"

The nine **months** of the school **year** fly by.

The last day has come. The students' minds are fat with knowledge. **Their** notebooks are rumpled from learning.

Thomas and the other children call out, "Thank you, Teacher."

She smiles and says, "Well done, my hard-working friends! See you next year."

Thomas and the other children race home.

The school is empty, and just in time.
The big rains have started.
The drops come down hard and fast.

Strong winds tear at the grass roof.

The rain finds its way inside.

The school's mud walls are soaked and start to slump.

The mud desks, too.

Slowly, the school disappears until there is almost nothing left.

It doesn't matter. The letters have been learned and the knowledge taken away by the children.

Come September, school will start over.
Thomas will be a big brother then, leading
the children on their first day to school.
They will all stand in front of their smiling
teachers, ready to build their school again.

Meet James Rumford

James Rumford says, "I have made books since I was a little boy. I drew the pictures and wrote the words. I still like doing that."

James has always loved to travel and see new places. At one time, he lived in Africa. The ideas for his books and illustrations come from the places he has been and the people he has met. Today, James lives in Hawaii.

Author's Purpose

James Rumford wanted to write about how the yearly rains affected the children of Chad. Draw a picture of yourself doing something outdoors. Write what the weather is like.

Respond to Reading

Retell

Use your own words to retell *Rain School*.

Text Evidence

1. Why do the children have to race home on the last day of school? **Cause and Effect**

2. In the end, what happens as a result of the heavy rain and strong winds? **Cause and Effect**

3. How can you tell that *Rain School* is realistic fiction? **Genre**

Make Connections

How does the weather in *Rain School* affect the children? **Essential Question**

Compare Texts
Read about how rain affects some people and places.

Rainy Weather

Weather changes from day to day. Some days are sunny, and some days are rainy. When it rains, do you wish the rain would go away? You might, but we need rain.

How Rain Helps

All living things need water. Rain helps
plants grow, so that people and animals
have food. Rain falls on ponds, lakes, and
rivers. Then animals can drink water all
year long. People need water to drink, too.
We also use it for cooking and cleaning.

Stormy Weather

We need rain, but rain can mean **storms,** and storms can mean problems. In a thunderstorm, thunder crashes! Lightning flashes! Lightning can strike trees or buildings.

A hurricane is a bigger storm. Heavy rains can cause a lot of **damage**. Winds can blow so hard that trees bend and break. There may be a flood. When it's over, people help each other clean it up.

Ready and Safe

Weather people can **predict** if a storm is on the way. Then we can stay safe.

In a thunderstorm or hurricane, the best place to be is inside. People may buy extra food, drinking water, and flashlights. Then they do not have to go outside. Soon the sun will be out. And then there will come another rainy day.

The red and yellow on this map show a storm.

Make Connections

How did the rain affect people in *Rain School*?
Essential Question

(bkgd) Ryan McVay/Lifesize/Getty images; (inset) NOAA

Essential Question

What traditions do you know about?

Read about a family tradition that helps a girl make friends.

Go Digital!

Lissy's Friends

by Grace Lin

Lissy was the new girl at school.

Nobody talked to her.
Nobody smiled at her.
At the playground, Lissy stood on the
merry-go-round by herself.

Because Lissy ate lunch alone, she was finished **before** lunchtime was over. Since she didn't have anything else to do, Lissy took the lunch menu in **front** of her and began to fold it. Soon, she had made a little paper crane.

"Hello," Lissy said to the paper crane. "I will call you Menu, and you will be my friend."

And to her surprise, Menu opened its eyes and blinked at her. Menu looked to the right, then to the left, and fluttered up with its paper wings.

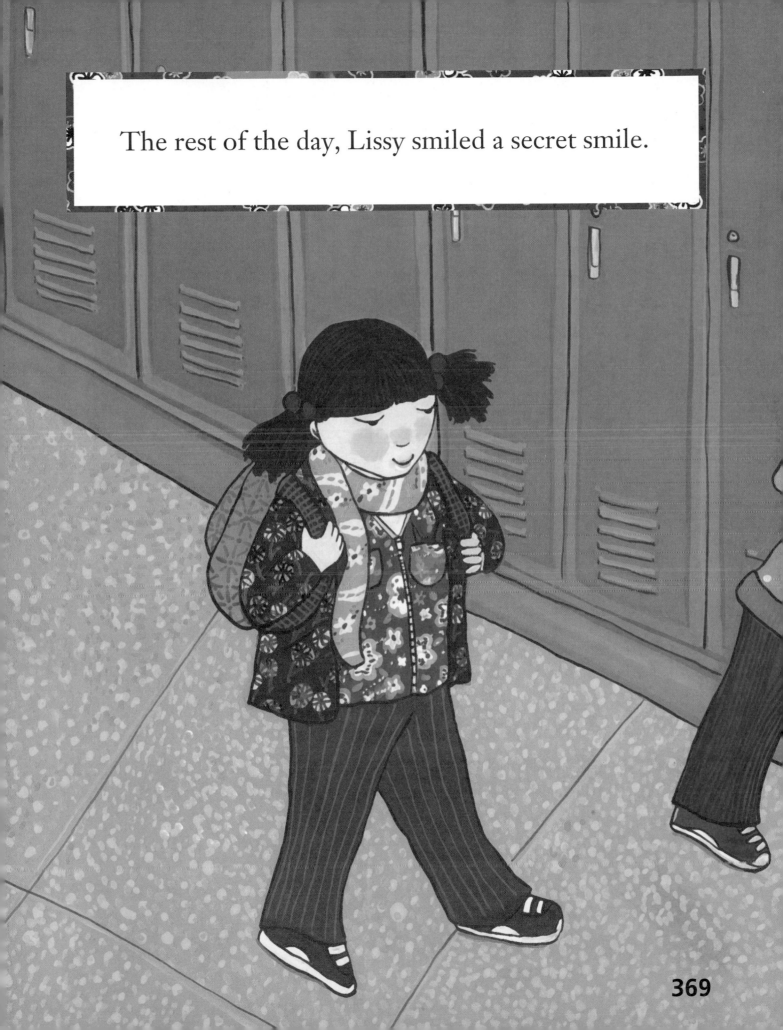

The rest of the day, Lissy smiled a secret smile.

"Did you make any friends in school today?" Mommy asked when Lissy came home.

"Well," Lissy said, patting Menu in her pocket, "I did make one friend."

"Good," Mommy said. "I'm sure you'll make more **tomorrow**."

And she did. The next day, Lissy made lots of friends.

373

Her friends went with her ...

everywhere.

And Lissy was never alone.

One day, Lissy **heard** a group of kids laughing as they went down the street. They stopped at onc house and then another, but they didn't stop at Lissy's.

"Lissy," Mommy called from downstairs, "why don't you go with **your** friends to the playground? I think they are all headed that way."

Lissy looked at her paper friends.

"Yes," shc said. "Let's go to the playground."

Lissy led her friends down the street and to the playground.

"We'll ride the merry-go-round first," she told them. "Then we can all ride together."

So all the paper animals crowded onto the merry-go-round, and Lissy began to **push** it. Round and round Lissy pushed. She ran so hard she didn't see that her friends were having a **difficult** time staying on ...

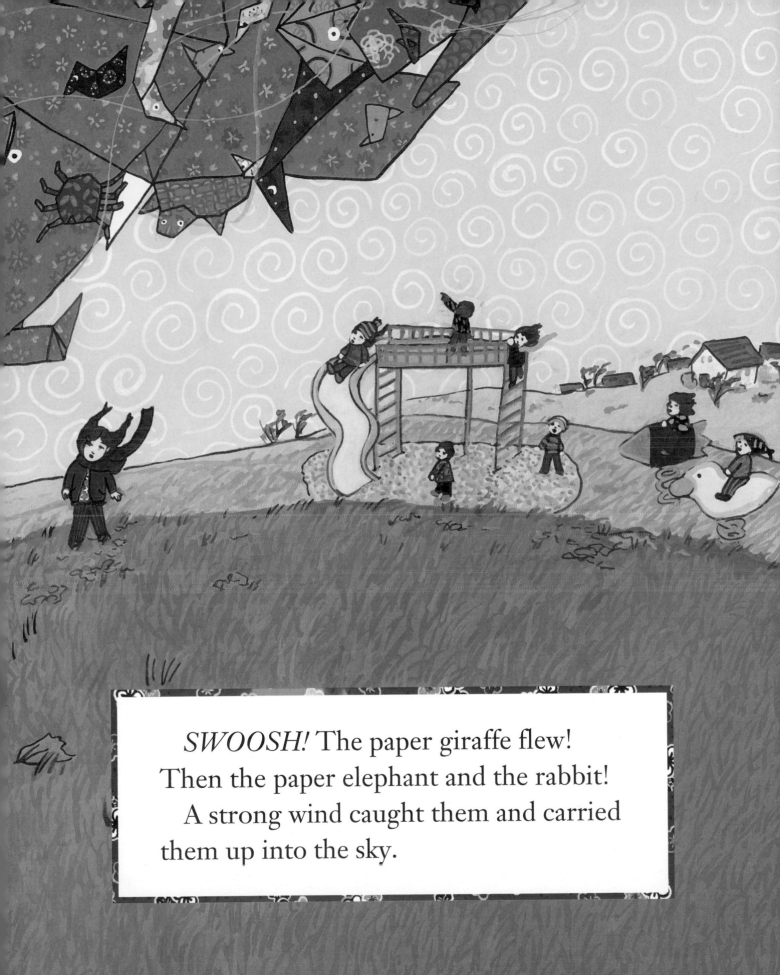

SWOOSH! The paper giraffe flew!
Then the paper elephant and the rabbit!
A strong wind caught them and carried
them up into the sky.

When Lissy jumped on, the merry-go-round was empty! She looked up and saw her paper friends flying away.

"No! Come back!" Lissy cried.

But they couldn't.

"No more friends," Lissy said, and she sat down on the merry-go-round and covered her face with her hands.

"Hey, is this yours?" a voice said.

Lissy looked up. There was a girl holding a paper crane. Menu!

"It's neat," the girl said. "Did you make it?"

Lissy looked at the girl. She was smiling at her. Lissy nodded.

"Can you show me how?" the girl asked. "I'm Paige."

Paige came over to Lissy's house, and Lissy showed her how to make a paper crane. Then they made a paper fox and dragonfly. They talked and laughed.

And the next day, Paige pushed Lissy on the
merry-go-round with lots and lots of friends.

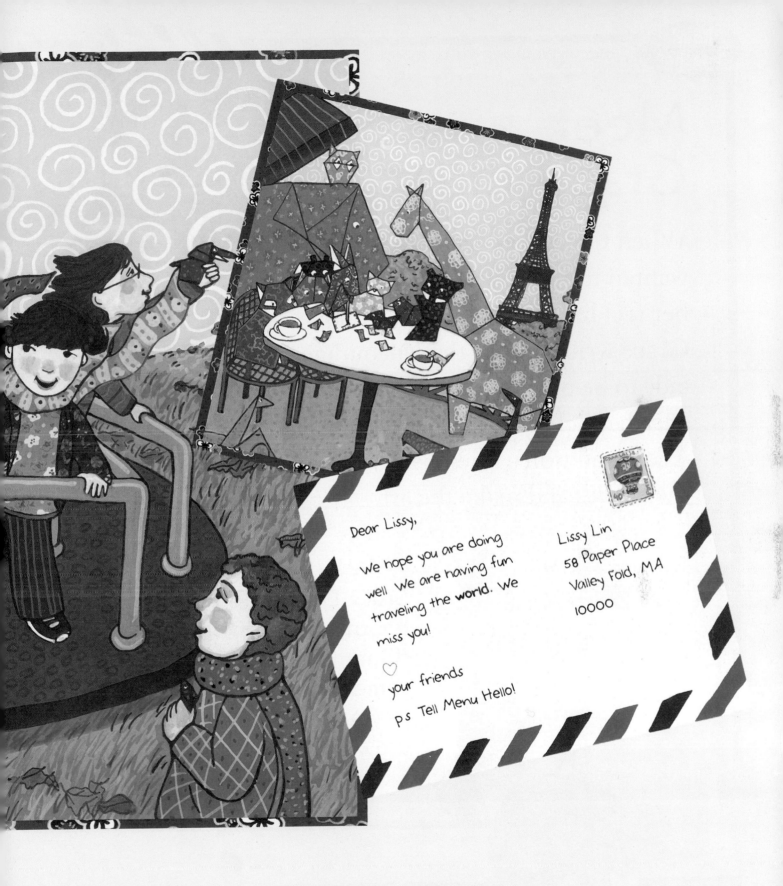

Dear Lissy,

We hope you are doing well. We are having fun traveling the **world**. We miss you!

♡

your friends

p.s. Tell Menu Hello!

Lissy Lin
58 Paper Place
Valley Fold, MA
10000

Meet Grace Lin

Dear Lissy,

We hope you are doing well. We are having fun traveling the world. We miss you!

♡
your friends

p.s Tell Menu Hello!

Lissy Lin
58 Paper Place
Valley Fold, MA
10000

When Grace was a child, she wanted to read books that made her feel like she belonged. So now, Grace writes books that encourage kids to be proud of their culture and that help readers appreciate Asian traditions. She likes to write the stories and make the art.

Author's Purpose

Grace Lin wanted to write about the tradition of making origami. Draw a picture of something that is a tradition in your family. Tell about your drawing.

Alexandre Ferron

Respond to Reading

Retell

Use your own words to retell *Lissy's Friends*.

Clue
↓
Clue
↓
Clue
↓
Theme

Text Evidence

1. How does Lissy make friends with the kids at her new school? **Theme**

2. What message does the author want the reader to understand? **Theme**

3. How can you tell that *Lissy's Friends* is realistic fiction? **Genre**

Make Connections

? What is a family tradition that you can share with others? **Essential Question**

Making Paper Shapes

See the crane made out of folded paper?
Folding paper to make different shapes is
called **origami**. People in Asia have made
origami for hundreds of years.

Kids learn this art from their mothers,
fathers, and grandparents.

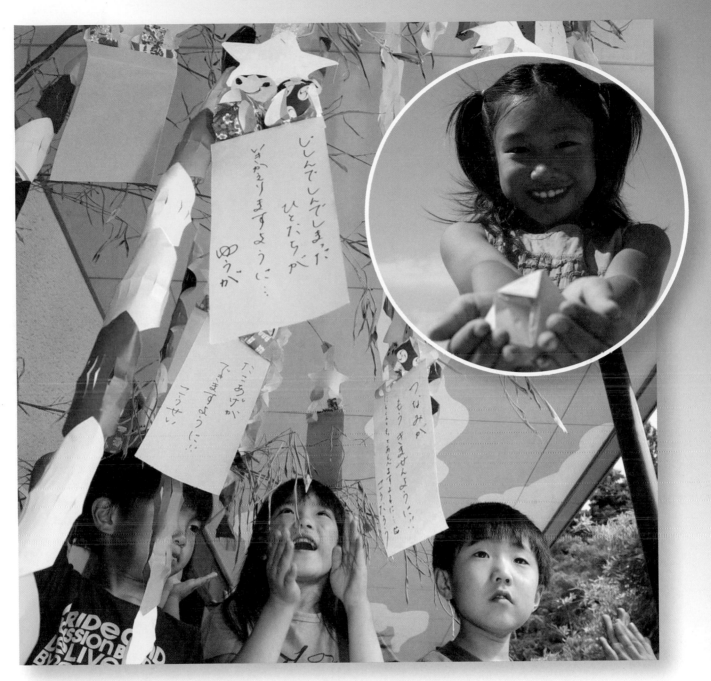

People in Japan make **decorations** for special days. One **holiday** is the Star Festival. Children sing songs and get treats to eat.

Families hang bright origami in the streets. Kids write wishes on slips of paper and hang them from sticks. They hope their wishes come true.

You can make origami, too. Use these directions to turn a square of paper into a cute dog.

1. Start with a square of paper. Fold it down in half so it forms a triangle.

2. Fold it in half again, like this. Press down the edge to make a crease.

3. Open the paper so you see a crease in the center.

4. Start from the crease and fold down both sides of the paper to make ears. See the dotted line? It shows you where to fold.

5. Now your dog will look like this.

6. Fold back the top of your dog so it is flat. Fold back the bottom so it is flat, too.

7. You made a dog! Now you can draw a face on it.

Make Connections
What might Lissy do with this dog? **Essential Question**

Steve Allen/Brand X Pictures

Essential Question

Why do we celebrate holidays?

Read about how our country began.

Go Digital!

Happy Birthday, U.S.A.!

Why do we celebrate the Fourth of July?

Whiz! Boom! Bang! That's the sound of fireworks that tear through the air. Colors light up the sky. Bands play and crowds roar. It's the Fourth of July!

Each year, people celebrate the birthday of the United States. It is a day for us all to share. We enjoy **favorite** things such as fireworks, parades, and picnics. This kind of party has **gone** on for over two hundred years. But how did this holiday begin?

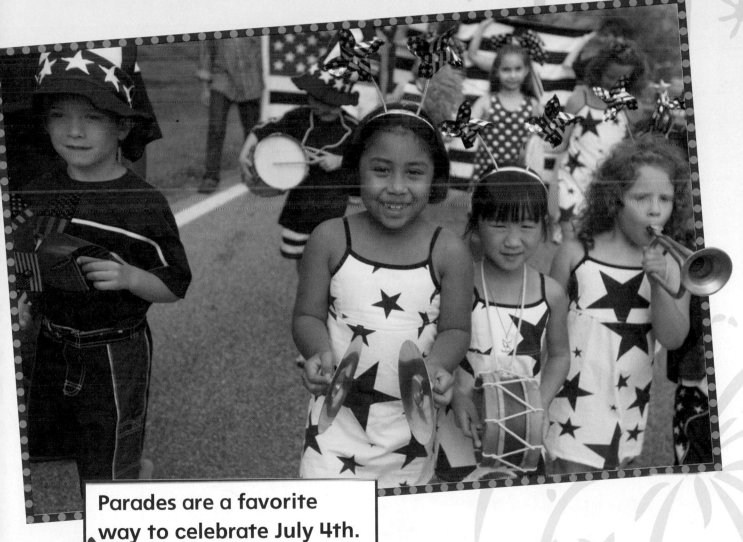

Parades are a favorite way to celebrate July 4th.

In 1775, our **nation** was small. It had just 13 colonies. A colony is like a state, but ruled by a leader far away. This ruler was the king of England. The people in the colonies did not like this. They felt the king's rules were not fair. They felt he did not care if they were happy.

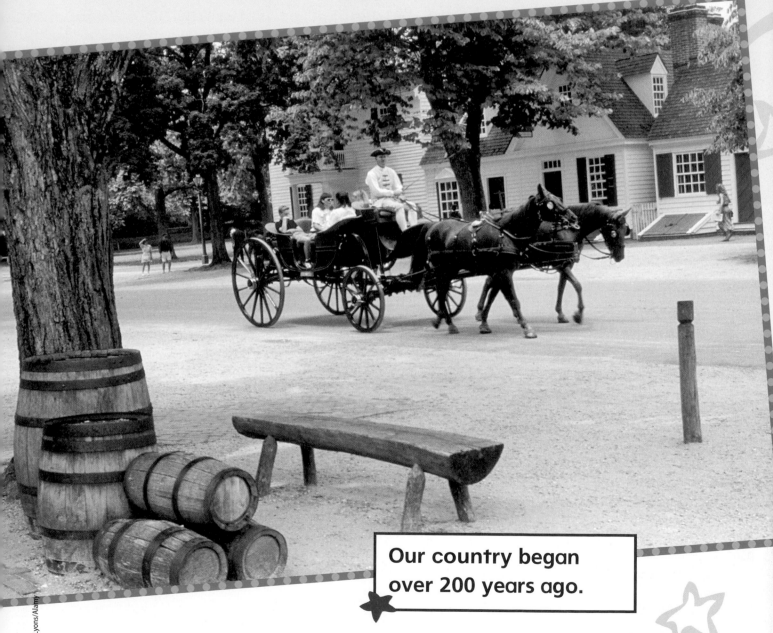

Our country began over 200 years ago.

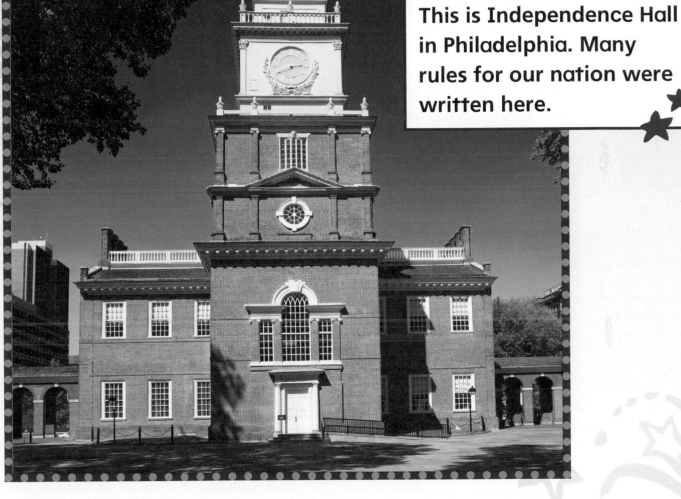

This is Independence Hall in Philadelphia. Many rules for our nation were written here.

On June 11, 1776, leaders of the **young** colonies met as a group called Congress. The people of the colonies wanted to split away from England. And the leaders wanted to **unite** to make new rules and write their own laws.

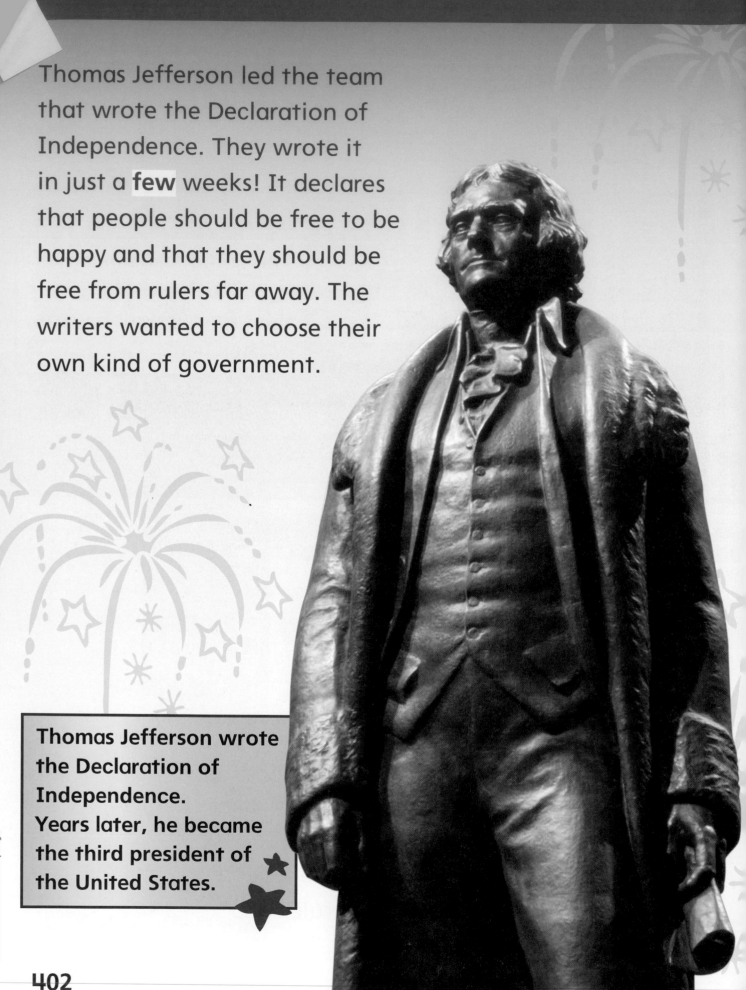

Thomas Jefferson led the team that wrote the Declaration of Independence. They wrote it in just a **few** weeks! It declares that people should be free to be happy and that they should be free from rulers far away. The writers wanted to choose their own kind of government.

Thomas Jefferson wrote the Declaration of Independence. Years later, he became the third president of the United States.

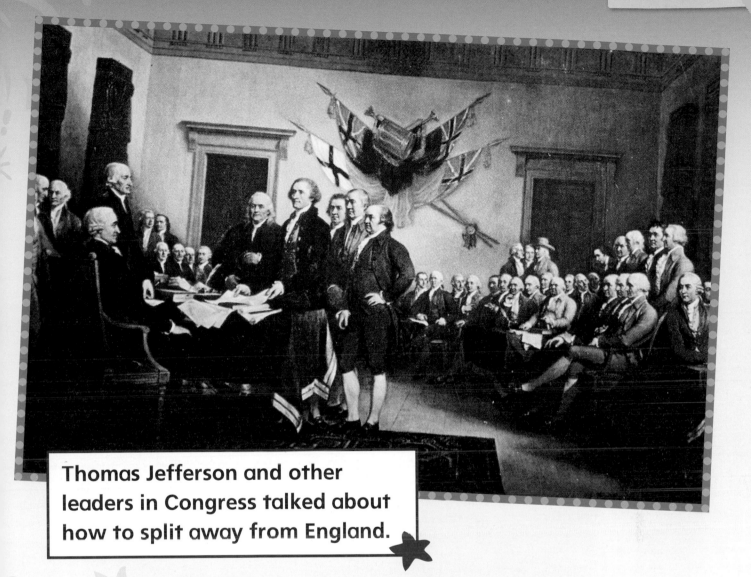

Thomas Jefferson and other leaders in Congress talked about how to split away from England.

Leaders started to sign the Declaration of Independence on July 4, 1776. They sent it to the king of England. He was **surprised** the colonies dared to do this. He did not want the colonies to be free.

The Declaration of Independence was first read out loud on July 4. Music blared and bells rang. One year later, fireworks lit up the sky on July 4.

This was just the beginning. It took a long fight for our nation to be free. But it would not have happened without the Declaration of Independence.

This is the Declaration of Independence. It told King George that the 13 colonies wanted to be free from England.

We celebrate our freedom and the declaration every year on the 4th of July. It's no **wonder** it is our nation's favorite holiday!

Respond to Reading

1. Why do you think the author wrote this piece? **Author's Purpose**

2. Why did the author tell about the king of England? **Author's Purpose**

3. How do you know that *Happy Birthday, U.S.A.!* is nonfiction? **Genre**

4. Why do we celebrate the Fourth of July? **Essential Question**

Compare Texts
Read about how the
13 colonies grew to
become the United States.

A Young Nation GROWS

In 1776, our nation had just
13 colonies. About 2 million
people lived here. Each colony
later became a state. Look
at the map of the colonies.
Read the colony names
below. Do you see any
names you know?

Philadelphia

1776
Colonies

The 13 Original Colonies

① Massachusetts
② New Hampshire
③ New York
④ Connecticut

⑤ Rhode Island
⑥ Pennsylvania
⑦ New Jersey
⑧ Maryland

⑨ Delaware
⑩ Virginia
⑪ North Carolina
⑫ South Carolina
⑬ Georgia

Illustration: Beth Griffis Johnson

Today, our nation has 50 states. More than 312 million people live here!

Did you know that Philadelphia was our nation's first capital?

What is our nation's capital today? If you guessed Washington, D.C., you are correct! It became the capital in 1790.

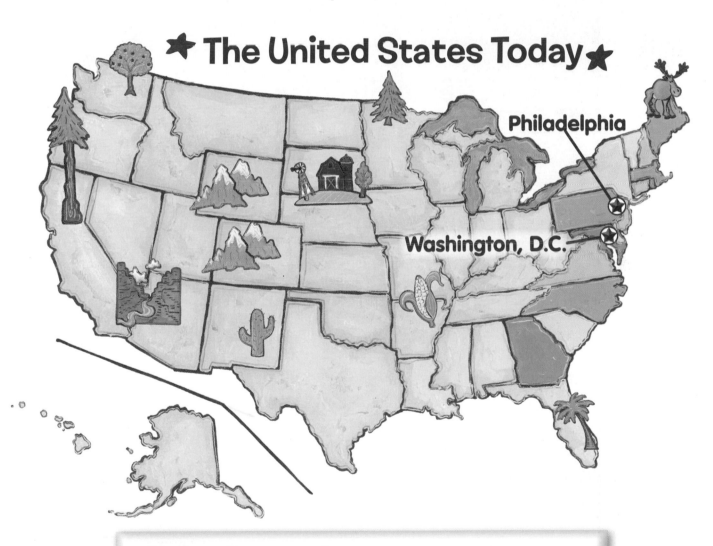

★ **The United States Today** ★

Philadelphia

Washington, D.C.

Make Connections

 What can you learn about the colonies from the map? **Essential Question**

Glossary

What is a Glossary? A glossary can help you find the meanings of words. The words are listed in alphabetical order. You can look up a word and read it in a sentence.

Sample Entry

Letter

Bb

Main Entry

Sentence

blue
The color of the sky is **blue**.

Aa

about
She likes to talk **about** her pet dog.

above
I saw the bird fly **above** the trees.

accept
Cal was happy to **accept** the gift.

animal
My favorite farm **animal** is a cow.

another
May I have **another** glass of water?

answer
Her **answer** to the question was yes.

Bb

balance
It is hard to **balance** on only one foot.

beautiful
The red flowers look **beautiful**.

because
Ty went to bed **because** he was tired.

been

I have never **been** on a plane.

before

Brush your teeth **before** you go to bed.

began

Our trip **began** on the bus.

better

Kim likes apples **better** than ice cream.

blue

The color of the sky is **blue**.

brother

I share a room with my older **brother**.

brought

Anna **brought** her lunch to school.

build

Jin likes to **build** things with blocks.

busy

Many cars drove on the **busy** road.

Cc

carry
Hope had to **carry** books to her classroom.

caught
I **caught** the ball in my baseball glove.

children
The **children** waved good-bye to their mom.

clever
The **clever** fox tricked the crow.

climb
Some cats like to **climb** up trees.

color
The **color** of my new dress is blue.

country
My friend moved to another **country**.

Dd

danger
A hot stove is a **danger** to a child.

demand

I **demand** that you return my pencil.

difficult

The problem was **difficult** to solve.

door

I lock the **door** when I leave the house.

Ee

early

Rosa wakes up **early** in the morning.

eight

All spiders have **eight** legs.

emergency

In an **emergency**, ask your parents for help.

enough

Sam had **enough** grapes, so he gave some to me.

eyes

I wear glasses to help my **eyes** see better.

Ff

fall
Cole saw the leaf **fall** from the tree.

fancy
The **fancy** house had many rooms.

father
My **father** walks me to school.

favorite
The dog's **favorite** toy is the red ball.

few
There are only a **few** pages left in the book.

find
Can you help me **find** my missing pencil?

flew
The plane **flew** high above the city.

food
I ate enough **food** for dinner.

found
Gwen **found** her socks in her shoes.

four

The kitten landed on all **four** of its legs.

friend

Brad asked his **friend** Emma to help him.

front

May I stand in the **front** of the line?

full

Rae's mom picked a lot of apples so her basket is **full**.

Gg

gathers

The blue jay **gathers** twigs for a nest.

give

I will **give** you a gift for your birthday.

gone

Ben has **gone** to his bedroom to sleep.

great

Nisha felt **great** after winning the race.

guess

Can you **guess** how many beans are in the jar?

Hh

hard
We studied **hard** for the test.

heard
We **heard** the bell and went into school.

Ii

idea
I will think of an **idea** for a new story.

instead
Will wants to read **instead** of play ball.

into
Joy watched the ducks dive **into** the lake.

Kk

knew
My mother **knew** how to get to the park.

know
I **know** that some sharks can swim quickly.

Ll

large
My dad's shoes were too **large** for my feet.

laugh
Jeb makes me **laugh** when he tells funny jokes.

leaped
The frog **leaped** into the pond.

learn
When I read books, I **learn** new words.

listen
Emily likes to **listen** to music.

love
I **love** my family because they take care of me.

Mm

money
Cass saved her **money** to buy new markers.

month

March is the **month** that comes before April.

more

A bucket holds **more** water than a cup.

mother

Her **mother** took care of her when she was ill.

Nn

nation

My friend comes from the **nation** of Mexico.

near

I sat **near** the sea to listen to the waves.

nobody

I rang the bell, but **nobody** was home.

none

None of the stores are open at night.

nothing

The empty box had **nothing** inside of it.

Oo

often

We went swimming **often** this summer.

oh

Oh! I didn't see you come in.

only

Ari wore the **only** coat he owned.

or

The family can have pasta **or** fish for dinner.

other

Nate likes this game more than the **other** one.

our

We gave **our** papers to the teacher.

over

A flock of birds flew **over** our heads.

Pp

partner

I asked Anya to be my **partner** for the game.

picture
Ray drew a **picture** with his pencil.

poor
The **poor** kitten lost its toy ball.

push
Paige had to **push** hard to open the door.

put
Please **put** the plates on the table.

Qq

question
My mom told me the answer to my **question**.

Rr

right
I know the **right** way to go home from school.

round
The **round** orange rolled off the table.

Ss

scrambled
The squirrel quickly **scrambled** down the tree.

search
They had to **search** for the missing keys.

section
I planted corn in one **section** of the garden.

seek
Snakes **seek** the sun to get warm.

signal
My coach gave a **signal** to start.

small
The **small** ladybug walked on the leaf.

special
My birthday is a **special** day for me.

splendid
Having a playdate is a **splendid** idea.

start
Start the race when you hear the whistle.

stretched
I **stretched** my arm to reach the top shelf.

suddenly
I awoke **suddenly** when I heard the loud noise.

sure
Are you **sure** that you want that one?

surprise
The party for my sister was a **surprise**.

Tt

their
The players had **their** team photo taken.

thought
I **thought** about the book after I read it.

through
The train went **through** the tunnel.

tomorrow
It is sunny today, but it will rain **tomorrow**.

toward
The puppy ran **toward** the house.

trouble
The class was in **trouble** for talking too much.

Uu

unite
Our team had to **unite** to beat the other team.

unusual
The cat had an **unusual** pattern on its fur.

Ww

warm
The baby had a bath in **warm** water.

were
We **were** at home all day.

whole
There were eight slices of pizza in
the **whole** pie.

woman
The **woman** carried her baby in
her arms.

wonder
I **wonder** how many stars are in the sky.

would
Tomás **would** like to be in the play.

write
I **write** my name at the top of the
paper.

Yy

year
There are twelve months in a **year**.

young
The **young** girl held her father's hand.

your
We can walk to **your** house.